HEADLINES

"Who? What? Where? Why? And when?"

HEADLINES:
an advanced text
for reading,
speaking,
and listening

Priscilla Karant
American Language Institute / New York University

Prentice-Hall, Inc., Englewood Cliffs, New Jersey 07632

Library of Congress Cataloging in Publication Data

Karant, Priscilla
  Headlines: an advanced text for reading, speaking,
and listening.

   1. English language—Text-books for foreign speakers.
2. College readers. I. Title.
PE1128.K34 1985   428.6′4   84-6864
ISBN 0-13-384744-6

Cover design: Ben Santora
Manufacturing buyer: Harry Baisley

The *New Yorker* cartoon on page 18 is by A. Levin, © 1981. The *New Yorker* cartoon on page 31 is by E. Koren, © 1982. The *New Yorker* cartoon on page 38 is by G. Booth, © 1977. The *New Yorker* cartoon on pages 74-75 are by A. Levin, © 1980. All *New Yorker* cartoons are copyrighted by The New Yorker Magazine, Inc.

© 1985 by Prentice-Hall, Inc., Englewood Cliffs, New Jersey 07632

Printed in the United States of America

10 9 8 7 6 5 4 3 2 1

ISBN 0-13-384744-6   01

Prentice-Hall International, Inc., *London*
Prentice-Hall of Australia Pty. Limited, *Sydney*
Editora Prentice-Hall do Brasil, Ltda., *Rio de Janeiro*
Prentice-Hall Canada Inc., *Toronto*
Prentice-Hall of India Private Limited, *New Delhi*
Prentice-Hall of Japan, Inc., *Tokyo*
Prentice-Hall of Southeast Asia Pte. Ltd., *Singapore*
Whitehall Books Limited, *Wellington, New Zealand*

To George and Nibo

Special thanks to Melinda Levine and Janis Schneider for their artwork; to Arnaldo Ramos for his photographs; to Larraine Fletcher for proofreading; and to Fred Malkemes for his voice and support. Thanks also to Florence Baskoff, Marcella Frank, and my family (especially Joshua) for all their encouragement and support. And of course thanks to all those wonderful students who inspired me.

Contents

Introduction

HEADLINES is a 14-unit book accompanied by a 30-minute tape that combines reading, vocabulary, listening, and speaking for advanced students of English as a second language. It can be used as the basic text for advanced classes in oral communication, listening comprehension, and reading skills. Each chapter includes a newspaper article selected for its lively approach to a modern topic, a simulated news broadcast that provides facts about the United States, and a variety of speaking and vocabulary exercises.

HEADLINES is designed to provide both the language tools necessary for good communication and the stimulus to use those skills in daily life. Its combination of reading, listening, and discussion centered around a single topic helps students integrate new ideas, vocabulary, and idioms into everyday speech. After students read an absorbing newspaper article that introduces new words and ideas, and then listen to a tape that presents a fresh perspective on the topic, they cannot wait to discuss their reactions in class and with neighbors. In their urgency to express their own views on a subject, they must master the language skills introduced moments before. In the process of making a viewpoint known and learning the viewpoint of others, the students make the language their own.

Below is an outline of the book and hints on how to use the material.

Reading the Article

Most students learning a new language are wedded to their dictionaries. They fear that if they do not look up every word, they will get hopelessly lost in the reading. They lose sight of what the author is trying to say and affix too much importance on the "unknown" words. Instead of focusing on the main ideas, students become mired in the minutest details.

To help the advanced student read more efficiently, the teacher should assure the student that some ambiguity is inevitable when one is reading a foreign language and this ambiguity will probably not interfere in one's understanding the thesis of the article. "Read for ideas, not for individual words" should be the slogan. The following instructions to the class help wean students from their dictionaries:

1. Try to read at the same speed as you read in your native language. Don't stop for new words on your first reading of the article.

2. On rereading, try to figure out the meaning of unfamiliar words from the context of the sentence. You'll be surprised how often you can avoid using a dictionary. Even if you can't figure out the exact meaning of a new word, determine what part of speech it is and what category of word it is. (The "Vocabulary in Context" exercise is designed to develop this skill.)

3. Most important, focus on understanding the main idea of the reading.

Test Your Reading Comprehension

EXERCISE A: TRUE/FALSE.   These true/false questions test the students' ability to understand the global ideas of the reading. This exercise can be assigned as homework, but the answers should be discussed in class. Have the class try to correct the false statements. When there is disagreement about the proper answer, have the students skim the article to locate the paragraph that supports their position.

EXERCISE B: IDENTIFY THE MAIN IDEA.   This exercise encourages the student to think about the author's purpose in writing the article. The main idea will always be a true statement. The student can also be asked to mark the paragraph(s) where the author has stated the main thesis.

EXERCISE C: VOCABULARY IN CONTEXT.   This first vocabulary exercise should be done with the entire class. The teacher should assist the class in analyzing the new word or phrase by reference to the context of the sentence.

For example, for a sentence such as "Every morning the child had granola, milk, and bananas for breakfast," how should students go about figuring out what "granola" means without using a dictionary? First, what part of speech is it? The students will tell you it's a noun. Second, what category of word is it (a means of transportation, an idea, a kind of food)? The students will tell you that it is probably food because milk and banana are food and the sentence said that the child had it for breakfast. After going through this, the class may still not realize that "granola" is a breakfast cereal eaten by Americans, but they do know enough so that the sentence is no longer bothersome.

The teacher should give students similar hints and choices to guide them through this exercise. Later in the semester this exercise can be done in small groups or in pairs. Students will catch on quickly and the exercise will become a game. Who can guess the closest? How did you figure it out? Of course, context clues are not limited to reading the individual sentence: the whole paragraph or reading is often useful for discovering the full meaning of a new word.

VOCABULARY 1 AND 2.   These exercises give the student an immediate opportunity to use the new vocabulary introduced in the story. From the context of the sentence, a student must choose the best word or the correct word form to fill in the blank. No dictionary should be used. The exercises can be assigned as homework and students can check their own answers.

VOCABULARY 3.   This is a written homework assignment in which students try out the new expressions. In class, the teacher should ask individuals to read their sentences aloud until several good examples are found. Students should then write down the clearest and most idiomatic use of each word or phrase.

VOCABULARY 4.   This exercise reviews some of the most frequent errors foreigners make in usage. How many times have you heard a student say that she or he is a "twenty-years-old" student? Some of these troublesome points are repeated throughout the book to correct the bad habits many advanced students still have.

Retell the Story

Students must orally reconstruct the story following the outline. The goal of the exercise is not to memorize the article but rather to incorporate the new vocabulary into a paraphrased recitation of the reading. This can be done in three steps:

1. The whole class tries to reconstruct the story with the teacher encouraging the use of new vocabulary.
2. To reinforce the vocabulary, each student retells the story in small groups or in pairs.
3. In a writing exercise, students can summarize the reading in their own words. This exercise can be assigned as homework.

The teacher should also elicit the reaction of the students to the story. This can be done orally or in writing.

Speak Up

These are varied activities for inside and outside the classroom to teach students to speak and listen more carefully. However, all of these exercises can be used as written exercises after presentation in class.

ONE-MINUTE SPEECH. This structured assignment builds a student's confidence in speaking in front of a group. The speech should be prepared and rehearsed at home. Students should not use notes while speaking and should strictly adhere to the time limit. In class the teacher can focus on a student's individual problems in grammar or pronunciation.

ROLE PLAY. This exercise allows the students to interact with classmates using idiomatic expressions. The teacher can again work on individual problems.

DEBATE. Many of the topics in HEADLINES raise controversial issues. Students should be encouraged to voice their opinions and respond to their opponents' views. Students not directly participating should be asked to take notes and ask questions at the end. Those involved in the debate should research the issue in the school library for facts to support their position.

Chart

Each chart is followed by questions to help students draw conclusions from the figures. Students should be encouraged to do research on the topic on their own and share their findings with the rest of the class.

Cartoons/Photographs

The student should describe in his or her own words what is going on in the cartoon or photograph. For example, who are the people in the picture? Where are they? What are they doing? Who is talking to whom? Can the student explain why the cartoon is supposed to be funny? That is, what is the unexpected thing about it that would make an American laugh? The students should be encouraged to bring in cartoons that they found to be of interest.

Listening

The listening exercise should proceed as follows:

1. Listen to the news broadcast without taking notes. (With a very advanced class, this step can be skipped. With a less advanced class, the students can go over the questions and vocabulary before listening to the tape.)
2. Listen again taking notes. (Students should never take notes in their native language. Only key words and phrases should be written down.)
3. Take the listening comprehension test. (Students should refer to their notes to answer these questions succinctly. A less advanced class should listen to the newscast twice.)
4. Go over the answers to the test.
5. Do Exercise B using the techniques outlined in the Vocabulary in Context exercise.
6. Listen to the tape for the final time. (By now the students will fully understand the main ideas of the news broadcast.)
7. Finally, do the Listening Carefully Exercise. (This is designed to teach students to hear series of words that are often slurred together in spoken English. The teacher can read the listening transcript paragraph as many times as necessary depending on the skill of the class. As the teacher reads the passage, students should fill in each blank with the missing words.)

Interview

These questions can be discussed in pairs, in small groups, or with the class as a whole. Encourage students to be as specific as possible in their responses. The teacher should visit each group or pair during these discussions to make sure the students are trying out the new vocabulary. At the end of the class the teacher can bring the students together as a whole and discuss any question of particular interest. These questions can also be used as one-minute speeches, telephone exercises, or writing exercises.

Telephone Exercises

Many of the speaking exercises, identified in the text with this symbol ☎ , provide the students with the opportunity to practice their conversational skills outside the classroom.

On the first day of class students should exchange telephone numbers, as well as the time of day they can be reached at that number. Students should be assigned to call each other at least once a week. A typical assignment will ask the student to exchange directions to his or her home with a fellow student. When the students return to class, they can check how accurately they gave and received directions.

The reason for an emphasis on telephone work is that most advanced English as a second language students still sound awkward and unsure of themselves on the telephone and complain of severe comprehension problems. High-level ESL students with complex vocabularies often make glaring mistakes when answering the telephone.

The instructions to the student, outlined on pages xvii–xix, provide familiar phrases used by native speakers on the telephone. Students should be encouraged to properly identify themselves on the telephone and to exchange pleasantries before rushing into the class assignment. Typical phrases for politely ending a telephone conversation are also listed.

In addition to these exercises, there are a wide variety of recorded messages that students can call on their own. Your local telephone company can tell you what types of recorded messages are available in your area, from daily weather and traffic reports to medical and consumer advice. These recorded telephone calls can be used as the basis for a One-Minute Speech. For example, a student can be assigned to call the weather forecast for that day and report it to the rest of the class.

Writing Ideas

While the main purpose of HEADLINES is to get students to overcome their fear of reading, speaking, and listening in English, many of the exercises in the book can be used to teach writing skills. Students can be assigned to write out any of the following:

—a summary of the reading
—a reaction to the reading
—any of the "Speak Up" exercises
—a summary of the listening transcript
—a transcript of the listening
—a reaction to the listening
—any of the answers to the "Interview" exercise
—a report on any current event related to the chapter

Using the Telephone: A Guide for Students

Speaking to your fellow students on the telephone will be part of the weekly homework assignment for this course. Your teacher will ask you to exchange telephone numbers with your classmates on the first day of class. Make sure you tell the other students the best time to call.

Making a phone call is difficult because you may not know the person you are talking to, you cannot see the person's face, the other party may be difficult to understand, and he or she may have problems understanding you. A working knowledge of American telephone language will go a long way to make phone conversations easier.

For example, every country has a different way of greeting a person on the phone:

> Our "hello" is the original Anglo-Saxon "be whole" or "be healthy." We use it in opening a telephone conversation, and so do many other tongues which have borrowed it from us. German, however, also uses "Here Mr. So-and-so." The British and Portuguese use "Are you there?" Spanish says "What is it?" or "At the phone." Italian says "Ready!" Russian says "I'm listening." Japanese says "If, if" the implication being "by all means speak up, if it is pleases you."[1]

Translating what you would say in your country into English may sometimes sound rude or confusing to an American. Instead of translating, learn American telephone language. It will facilitate all your phone conversations.

[1]Mario Pei, *The Story of Language* (New York: New American Library, 1964) pp. 71–72.

OPENING THE CONVERSATION (THE CALLER)

—Hello, may I please speak to Mr. Lee?
—Hello, could I please speak to Mrs. Rodriguez?
—Hello, I'd like to speak to Mr. Taru.

ASKING FOR IDENTIFICATION (PERSON BEING CALLED)

—Who's calling please?
—Who is this, please?
—Who(m) would you like to speak to?

IDENTIFYING YOURSELF (THE CALLER)

—This is Mr. Park
—This is Mrs. Azia speaking.
—This is Mr. Levy calling.
—This is he (she).

ASKING SOMEONE TO REPEAT

—I'm sorry (excuse me, pardon me), what did you say?
—Could you please slow down? I'm having trouble following you.
—Would you mind repeating that?
—How do you spell that? Would you mind spelling that?
—I didn't catch what you said.

TOO BUSY TO TALK

—Is this a good time to call? I hope I'm not interrupting anything.
—I'm in the middle of something. Can I call you back right away?
—I was just about to leave. Can I call you later?
—I was on my way out. How about calling back in an hour?
—I'm tied up at the moment. When is a good time to catch you?
—Let me take down your number. I'll call you right back.

ENDING A CONVERSATION (THE CALLER)

—Well, it's been good talking to you.
—I'd better let you go.
—Thanks for your time.
—I appreciate your help.
—I've really enjoyed talking to you.
—I hope to speak to you (hear from you) soon.
—Speak to you soon.

ENDING A CONVERSATION (THE PERSON BEING CALLED)

—Well, thanks for calling.
—It was really good to hear from you.
—Give me a call if you have any more questions.

—Let me know if I can be of any further help.

—Feel free to call again.

Many students also have problems dealing with the local telephone company. Here are some typical requests for assistance:

CALLING THE OPERATOR

—Can you give me the area code for San Francisco?

—What is the number for information in Manhattan?

—I'd like to make a person-to-person call to Mr. Lee. The number is area code 201 777-8932.

—I'd like to make a collect call to area code 201 777-8932. My name is Ms. Rodriguez.

—I'd like to make a long distance phone call and charge it to my home phone.

CALLING THE OPERATOR ABOUT TELEPHONE TROUBLE

—I've been dialing this number for one hour and it's always busy. I think there is something wrong with the line. Could you check the number, please?

—I was cut off while talking. Could you reconnect me and give me credit for my call?

—There was so much static on the line that I couldn't hear the other party. Could you reconnect me please and give me credit for the call?

—I just called the wrong number. Can you give me credit please?

—I just lost a quarter in the phone booth. Can you give me credit please?

—I'm having trouble getting through to this number. Could you help me, please?

1 **Chinese Accountants Find That America Is Hard to Figure**

What is commonplace in one country may startle a visitor from another country. Surely you have experienced this feeling yourself when traveling. Sociologists call this universal phenomenon "culture shock." The following article tells what happened to four Chinese accountants on their first visit to the United States.

CHINESE ACCOUNTANTS FIND THAT AMERICA IS HARD TO FIGURE

By DEAN ROTBART

CLEVELAND— Li Shuang got his first taste of Western culture recently: cold oil-and-vinegar soup. He also wrestled with an elevator and was locked inside a car.

Mr. Li, a 37-year-old Peking accountant, along with three of his colleagues—Ke Ming and Li Yong, both 29 years old, also from Peking, and Tang Yun Wei, 37, of Shanghai—came to the U.S. last month to study American accounting and auditing methods. Their objective is to learn the U.S. system well enough so that when they return to the People's Republic of China, in about a year, they can help improve the system there.

Ernst & Whinney, the Cleveland-based accounting firm, is sponsoring the sojourn of Mr. Li and his three companions. Its hospitality is part of an arrangement worked out last fall, when the firm agreed to be host to four Chinese citizens: two each for rotating six month stints in its Cleveland and Chicago offices. In return, Peking permitted Ernst & Whinney to have a U.S. partner reside in China.

First Assignment

The four Chinese men's first assignment in the U.S. was a one-week orientation (you should pardon the expression) on the way Americans eat, work, and play. They handled themselves about as well as, say, four Americans in Shanghai. While they endured the rigors of the week with relatively few scars—this reporter tagged along as an observer for most of the week—it is unlikely that they will return home extolling the American way of life to their countrymen.

"I think I'm glad to be a Chinese," Mr. Li said before his first week in America was over.

The culture shock of modern America hit even before the four visitors arrived in the U.S. When Mr. Li's first Western meal was served on the plane from Peking to San Francisco, the main course, side dishes and soft drinks were all, understandably, foreign to him. Most puzzling, however, were the glass of cold water and the small cup of salad dressing that came with the meal tray.

Having no familiarity with American salads, Mr. Li assumed the oil and vinegar was a soup mix. He poured it into the water and drank the entire concoction. "It wasn't very delicious," he recounted upon his arrival.

A Grape Disappointment

All four men speak English, but their fluency is limited, as is their knowledge of Western ways. They address a hotel restaurant waitress as "maid," much to her chagrin. Mr. Tang orders grapefruit for breakfast and is unhappy to be served what he calls "a

2

sour orange" instead of the grapes he thought he would get. Mr. Ke says he is looking forward to seeing American movies, although, he adds suavely, he already has seen several in China, including " 'Son of Music' and 'Snow White and the Four Dwarfs.' "*

Throughout their first week in Cleveland, it was American food and the rituals associated with eating it that posed the greatest challenges to the Chinese men. Mr. Ke, at a reception the evening of his arrival, wanted to demonstrate to his American hosts his mastery of the fork, which Chinese people seldom see, much less use.

With lines of concentration forming on his forehead, Mr. Ke grasped the fork handle tightly and slicing into a wedge of cantaloupe with the side of the fork, sent the several pieces of melon whirling off his plate onto the floor. His first lesson in the American art of blushing was a success.

The Chinese men claimed they liked American food, greeting each new dish with such comments as "marvelous" and "very, very good." In fact, they dreaded every bite of some dishes.

"To tell the truth," Li Yong confessed after a welcome reprieve of a Chinese meal one evening, "I don't like Western food." When asked how he expected to manage a year in this country under those circumstances, he pondered for a moment, then he replied, "I'll eat rice." Li Yong said that blue cheese dressing tastes like "rotten soybean cake." Mr. Tang quizzed an American at lunch one day about possible excuses he could use to refuse food without offending his hosts. The one he fancied most was: "It doesn't agree with me."

*Do you know the real names of these movies? "The Sound of Music" and "Snow White and the Seven Dwarfs." (Editor's note).

Li Yong had acquired a notion about the way Americans sell groceries. "I read a rumor in a Chinese newspaper that they sell dog food in American supermarkets," he confided with some hesitation, clearly concerned that his query not be misconstrued to suggest he endorsed such malicious gossip.

When told that supermarkets indeed sell dog food, Li Yong couldn't suppress his laughter or hide his astonishment. "Oh, oh, it's true. It's unbelievable!" he exclaimed. "The dogs and cats in America eat better than people in Asian countries." In China, Li Yong said, dogs aren't ordinarily kept as pets; they have to fend for themselves and are more likely to be eaten than to enjoy a good meal.

The Two-Door Policy

Some American doors puzzled the four men. After becoming acquainted with Ernst & Whinney's educational training center, where the formal orientation was held, Mr. Ke observed: "The men's room there is very different. Two doors. One in and one out. There are too many new things to learn at once."

On one occasion, a frustrated and somewhat embarrassed Li Shuang found himself securely locked in the far rear seat of a station wagon. For some reason, the back door wouldn't open. Several Ernst & Whinney people finally instructed him to crawl over the middle seat and go out a side door. He came out vowing, "I'll never forget that."

Within an hour, Mr. Li had another run-in with a door. This time, in a gesture of typical Chinese courtesy, he used his body to prop open an elevator door so that those inside could get off. The door had different

Continued on Page 4, Column 1

ideas, however, and repeatedly bat-
tered him in the side. Although he
maintained a stoic smile, he walked
165 away from the elevator mumbling in
his native tongue.

Spacious Apartment

The apartment that Ernst & Whinney rented for the men in Cleveland is
170 a two-bedroom, spacious suite on the
14th floor of a downtown highrise. The
men obviously liked the two private
bathrooms, a considerable improvement over the communal commodes
175 used in China. Together, the bathrooms alone are about half as large as
Mr. Tang's Shanghai residence, he
indicated, looking incredulously at
the master bath.
180   The rental agent for the building
rattled on and on about the garbage
disposal and dishwasher, oblivious to
the uncomprehending looks on the
Chinese men's faces. "You mean they
185 don't know what ice-cube trays are?"
the aghast rental agent asked, after an
Ernst & Whinney employee explained
that her long discourse on the function and operation of various appli-
190 ances was lost on the men.
Many of the questions the men
raised proved difficult for the Ernst &
Whinney people to answer. After listening to advice about tipping, Li Yong
wanted to know why, if Americans 195
want better service, they don't tip barbers or waiters before they perform
their services rather than after. "That
makes sense," admitted Theodore J.
Krein, an Ernst & Whinney manager 200
who helped organize the visitor's orientation, "but we don't do that."
At the Cleveland Public Library, a
large modern painting entitled "Night
Sky: Cleveland" stopped Li Yong in his 205
tracks. "I can't understand it. What is
it?" he asked, pointing to the jumbled
mixture of blacks, dark blues, and
other colors on a gray background.
Neither the library guide nor the Ernst 210
& Whinney people on the tour
answered, and instead directed his
attention to the periodicals room.
Soon the four men's days will
be filled with generally accepted 215
accounting principles and other such
stuff. But for the next year their eyes
and ears also will be taking in the life
of America that unfolds around them.
"Old saying in America: Seeing is 220
believing," Mr. Ke says. "Some people
say America is very beautiful, and
some say otherwise. So now I will have
a chance to see with my own eyes."

TEST YOUR READING COMPREHENSION

A.   Based on the reading, decide whether the following statements are true or false.

1. The Chinese accountants came to the United States to learn about American food and apartments.
2. The Chinese accountants only pretended to like American food.
3. Some Americans eat cold oil-and-vinegar soup.
4. The author thinks that Americans in Shanghai would have as many problems as the Chinese accountants had in Cleveland.
5. Some people in China eat dogs.
6. The Chinese accountants felt that the American system of tipping made sense.

7. The hotel waitress likes to be called "maid."
8. The Chinese accountant enjoyed his grapefruit.
9. The Chinese accountants experienced culture shock on their first trip to Cleveland.

B.   Which of the sentences above best states the main idea of the reading? Circle it.

C.   *Vocabulary in Context:* Without using a dictionary, study how the following words or phrases are used in the reading. Work together in pairs to figure out what the words mean.

(20) sojourn
(28) reside
(39) tagged along
(41) extolling
(92) whirling off
(107) pondered
(122) query
(159) prop open
(181) rattled on

D.   *Vocabulary 1:* Fill in the blanks with the correct word.

dreaded	misconstrued	reprieve	vowed
gossip	mumbled	stoic	
grasp	oblivious	suppress	

1. _____ to the noise around him, he kept on studying.

2. We couldn't hear what she said because she _____ .

3. He was a real _____ who never showed how much he was suffering.

4. She _____ she would never do it again.

5. It was so funny that we could hardly _____ our laughter.

6. He's always spreading _____ about the other employees.

7. Dinner was a welcome _____ from the boring speeches.

8. He _____ going to the dentist although he had a toothache.

9. The student didn't _____ the meaning of the story.

10. The politician claimed his comments were _____ because he was quoted out of context.

E.   *Vocabulary 2:* Fill in the blanks with the correct word form.

1. **(true)**   Tell me the _____ !

2. (puzzle)   The new immigrants found American customs

     _____ .

3. (succeed)   Their trip was quite a _____ .

4. (fluency)   He was _____ in three languages.

5. (embarrass) To make mistakes in English is very _____ .

6. (endure)   After passing the two-hour _____ test, she
                was declared qualified to be a firefighter.

7. (rigor)   To become a soldier, he had to go through a

                _____ training period.

8. (assume)   You don't have any facts to support your

                _____ .

F.   *Vocabulary 3:* Write your own sentence using the italicized phrase.

1. They address a hotel restaurant waitress as "maid," *much to her chagrin.*
2. Mr. Ke says he is *looking forward to* see*ing* American movies.
3. Dogs aren't ordinarily kept as pets; they have to *fend for themselves.*
4. A large modern painting entitled "Night Sky: Cleveland" *stopped* Li Yong *in his tracks.*
5. After *becoming acquainted with* Ernst & Whinney's educational training center, Mr. Ke observed: "The men's room there is very different."
6. Its hospitality is part of an arrangement *worked out* last fall.

G.   *Vocabulary 4:* These words are often misused. Choose the correct word and explain your choice.

1. They endured the rigors of the week with relatively (**a few, few**) scars.
2. This reporter tagged along as an observer for (**most, the most, almost**) of the week.
3. The culture shock of modern America hit even before the four visitors arrived (**at, in, to**) the United States.
4. After (**listening, hearing**) to (**advice, advise**) on tipping, Li Yong wanted to know why, if Americans want better service, they don't tip barbers or waiters before they perform their services.
5. Soon the four men's days will be filled with generally accepted accounting (**principals, principles**) and other such stuff.
6. The apartment rented for the men is a (**two-bedroom, two-bedrooms**), spacious (**suit, suite**) (**in, on**) the 14th floor.

RETELL THE STORY

Use the outline below ás a guide to retell the story in class.

- why the Chinese accountants are in America
- the first Western meal on the airplane
- their problems in the restaurant (maid, grapefruit, fork)
- their reaction to the supermarkets (American food, dog food)
- the station wagon story
- the elevator door problem
- the spacious apartment
- the modern painting

SPEAK UP

1. ONE-MINUTE SPEECH: What are the "do's" and the "don'ts" for an American going to your country? Give some sound advice. Be as specific as possible about the particular customs of your country relating to greetings, food, dress, and body language. For example, can you wear shorts in public in your country? Can you eat certain foods with your fingers? Should you remove your shoes before entering someone's home?

2. ROLE PLAY: *American Host and Foreign Guest.* You have been invited to eat dinner at the home of an American friend. You will be offered various kinds of food and drinks that you think you won't like. Politely refuse. The host will urge you to reconsider because "it was made especially for you." Change your mind and give the new food a try. Use the expressions below.

REFUSING

It doesn't agree with me.
I don't especially (particularly) care for . . . .
I'd much rather have . . . .
Do you have any . . . .
If you don't mind, I'll have _____ instead.
Well / Actually / Honestly / Frankly / To tell the truth . . . .
I'm full (stuffed).

URGING SOMEONE TO EAT

Please help yourself.
Have another bite (sip, piece, drink).
Do taste it.
You don't know what you're missing.
I made it especially for you.

CHANGING YOUR MIND

Well, if that's so, I'll take a bite.
On second thought, I'll try some.
When you put it that way, I'd love to taste it.

3. INTRODUCTIONS:
   A. What is the proper way to introduce a friend to someone? Is it polite to ask a stranger about: age, height, job, company, marriage status, health, religion, children, telephone number, address? Discuss it with your classmates. Then act out a typical introduction scene.
   B. Find out the name and background of the person sitting next to you. Pretend you are at a party with a new friend whom you want everyone to meet. Stand up and circulate around the room, greeting old friends and introducing your new companion. Use the expressions below.

   EXPRESSIONS

   Gee, it's good to see you.
   It's been a long time.
   What have you been up to?
   What's new?
   I'd like to introduce you to a very good friend of mine.
   I'm very pleased to meet you.
   I've heard a lot about you.
   It's been good talking to you.

4. DEFINE SOME OF THESE POPULAR SAYINGS: How many of these sayings do you know? Can you explain to the rest of the class what they mean? Give specific instances when it would be appropriate to use them. What others do you know?

   Seeing is believing.
   Better late than never.
   The grass is always greener on the other side.
   People in glass houses shouldn't throw stones.
   Don't count your chickens before they hatch.
   His bark is louder than his bite.
   If you give him an inch, he'll take a mile.
   A stitch in time saves nine.
   A bird in the hand is worth two in the bush.
   Too many cooks spoil the broth.
   Don't cry over spilled milk.

TABLE 1-1   Temporary Visitors to the United States

MAJOR VISA CATEGORIES		
A	Foreign government officials	83,800
B-1	Business travelers	800,000
B-2	Tourists	6,642,700
F-1	Students	187,100
F-2	Students' spouses and children	19,700
J-1	Exchange visitors	53,000
L-1	Intracompany transferees	21,000

Refer to Table 1-1 in answering the following questions.

1.   What visa group accounts for the largest number of visitors?
2.   What kind of visa did you have when you first came to the United States? Can you find it listed above? If not, explain what type of visa you had.
3.   What kind of visa do you think the Chinese accountants had?

TABLE 1-2   Where Do the New Immigrants in the United States Come From Today?

Africa	2.6%
Asia	41.4%
Canada	3.0%
Europe	13.4%
Latin America	38.6%
Oceania	1.0%

Refer to Table 1-2 in answering the following questions.

1.   What two regions make up the largest source of new immigration to the United States?
2.   What factors might have contributed to this?

TABLE 1-3   Average Yearly Immigration to the United States

1980	808,000 (estimated)	1930–39	69,938
1970–79	446,518	1920–29	429,551
1960–69	321,375	1910–19	634,738
1950–59	249,927	1900–09	820,239
1940–49	85,661		

Refer to Table 1-3 in answering the following questions.

1.   In which decade since 1900 did the United States receive the fewest number of immigrants?
2.   What worldwide event occurred during that decade?

TEST YOUR LISTENING
COMPREHENSION

A. Listen to the tape before going on. (The Listening Transcript appears on page 129.) Based on the listening, answer the following questions.

1. How many legal immigrants arrive each year in the United States?
2. When did many Europeans migrate to the United States?
3. What proportion of the immigrants come from Asia?
4. What proportion of the immigrants come from Latin America?
5. What proportion now come from Europe?
6. Compared with other nations, how many immigrants does the United States accept?
7. How many illegal immigrants come each year?
8. What have several congressmen proposed to solve this problem?
9. How do some business groups and civil rights leaders feel about this proposal?

B. Listen to the newscast again for these words. Can you guess their meaning from the context?

mass migration
turn of the century
a new ceiling
knowingly hire
heavy fine
wholesale discrimination

C. *Listening Carefully:* Your teacher will read aloud the following passage. Fill in the blanks with the missing words.

The latest figures from the United States Immigration and Naturalization

Service show that _____ one million immigrants are now
                          (1)

_____ America every year. This is _____ number of
        (2)   (3)

newcomers _____ since the mass migration of Europeans
                    (4)

_____ turn of the century. The new immigrants no longer come
        (5)

mainly from Europe. According to the official _____ estimate,
                                                              (6)

_____ source of _____ to America is now Asia,
        (7)   (8)

_____ Latin America.
        (9)

INTERVIEW

Use these questions as a guide to interview a classmate. Add questions of your own.

1. What American customs surprised you the most when you first came to the United States? Be specific.

2. Describe a funny incident that happened to you in America because you didn't know English well.

3. Do you feel that Americans are more impolite than people in your country? What makes you think so? Describe an incident.

4. Do foreigners "stick out" in your country? What do they do that makes it evident that they are foreign? Describe their behavior. For example, what is the stereotype of an American tourist in your country?

5. What is the stereotype foreigners have of people from your country? How accurate do you think it is?

2 Cairo Tightens Lax Approach to Driver Test

No country in the world seems to be immune from traffic tie-ups and costly accidents. The way people drive cars in Cairo may make you laugh, but automobile accidents are no joke. Here is the story of how Egypt is dealing with this problem.

CAIRO TIGHTENS LAX APPROACH TO DRIVER TEST

By CHRISTOPHER S. WREN

CAIRO— Dec. 8—It was examination time at the shabby department office in the Giza suburb of Cairo. License applicants waited nervously
5 to demonstrate their proficiency by driving forward, then backing up and parking alongside a white line painted on the asphalt.

As spectators kibitzed, a middle-
10 aged matron edged her sedan cautiously ahead. Not knowing how to shift into reverse, she had hired a small boy to push the car backward. The inspector advised her to return
15 after a week and try again.

A confident young man squealed to a stop, propelled his Fiat backward in a cloud of dust, and wound up perpendicular to the white line. He
20 flunked too.

The only requirement for an Egyptian driver's license used to be knowing how to put the car in gear. A Cairo resident who took his test several
25 years ago recalled taking along a carload of friends, who were also awarded licenses by the amiable inspectors.

Standards Were Tightened

30 The standards are tougher now. In the Attabe traffic office of central Cairo, applicants must perform a series of turns. Until recently in Giza, they had to back between two rubber
35 traffic cones. Apparently because of high cone attrition, this was changed to the painted white lines.

Drivers must also present doctors' certificates attesting to good
40 health and vision, though the applicants have been known to send their doormen out to have the forms done. They must also identify traffic symbols from a plastic-covered chart, held
45 upside down when this reporter took the test.

But drivers are not tested on how to behave on the road, and there are few deterrents to recklessness. Poor
50 discipline, ineffectual law enforcement, and rattletrap vehicles contribute to some notorious traffic jams.

It is not unusual in Cairo for drivers to cruise up one-way streets the
55 wrong way, disregard traffic lights, abruptly swerve right from left-hand lanes, and park on the sidewalks. Turn signals are seldom used; seat belts, never. Kasr el-Nil and Sarwa streets in
60 central Cairo become so clogged with double and triple parking that moving traffic must compete for the one remaining lane.

Fines Paid with License Renewal

65 The drivers keep doing it because they never get punished on the spot. Instead, policemen write down the license numbers of offending cars and the fines, from 70 cents to $7, are
70 added to the annual license renewal.

This has hardly inhibited bad driving. In the neighborhood of Zamalek the other day a stream of cars made a particularly popular U-turn in front of
75 a lone policeman, who could not jot down the license numbers fast enough.

Continued on Page 14, Column 1

13

At Galaa Square a sedan forged on through a red light, dodging a policeman who heroically tried to interpose himself in the intersection.

Of the 250,000 motor vehicles that vie with pedestrians and push-carts in Cairo's crowded streets, 170,000 are private cars. Nabil Halawa, chairman of the Public Transport Authority, disclosed this fall that private cars represented only 4 percent of Cairo's population, which exceeds 8 million people. The other 96 percent make do on overloaded buses and trams.

Mr. Halawa called this imbalance "a situation that is very hard to believe, yet it is true." But his proposal that the cars be confined to side streets on weekdays to make more room for public transport has not met with visible enthusiasm.

Cars Reflect Rich—Poor Gap

The crush of automobiles has accentuated the gap between rich and poor. David Gurin, Deputy Transportation Commissioner for New York City, visited Egypt last winter and noticed "a class struggle in the streets of Cairo between the people who have automobiles and those who don't."

Mr. Gurin said at a seminar here that "in few places have I ever felt as swimming in transportation as I have here."

While New York and Cairo are roughly the same size in population, he observed, Cairo has only half as many buses and no subway.

Last spring, the Ministry of Transport and Communications issued a report admitting that Egypt had the world's highest death rate for road accidents. The report said that for every 1,000 cars in Egypt, 2.049 persons were killed annually, which is ten times the rate for Britain.

The snail's pace of Cairo traffic has kept fatalities down, but mangled automobiles are a common sight.

Attempts to reduce the congestion have included the construction of overpasses and some confusing experiments with one-way arteries.

TEST YOUR READING COMPREHENSION

A. Based on the reading, decide whether the following sentences are true or false.

1. It's harder than it used to be to get a driver's license in Cairo.
2. One woman hired a small boy to take the test for her.
3. Parking the car used to be the only thing you had to do to pass the driving test.
4. Several years ago, a Cairo resident bribed an inspector so that all his friends would be awarded licenses.
5. Even though the driver's test is tougher, traffic in Cairo is still very bad.
6. Speeding motorists are one of the main reasons for the traffic problems in Cairo.
7. The Cairo police make many arrests for traffic violations.
8. The traffic in Cairo is congested because most people drive to work.

9.   There are proportionately more traffic fatalities in Egypt than in Britain.

10.   Many cars in Cairo have dents from accidents.

B.   Which of the sentences above best states the main idea of the reading? Circle it.

C.   *Vocabulary in Context:* Without using a dictionary, study how the following words or phrases are used in the reading. Work together in pairs to try to figure out what the words mean.

(8) asphalt
(9) kibitzed
(16) squealed to a stop
(35) cones
(56) swerve
(73) a stream of
(78) forged on
(81) interpose
(125) the snail's pace
(129) mangled

D.   *Vocabulary 1:* Fill in the blanks with the correct word.

clogged	dodge	ineffectual	tougher
cruise	fatally	reckless	
deter	flunked	shabby	

1.   Since he's been unemployed, his face is unshaven and his clothes look

_____ .

2.   Many feel that parents should be _____ on their unruly children.

3.   What will _____ him from leading a life of crime?

4.   She won't go in the car with him because he's such a _____ driver.

5.   Call the plumber because the sink is _____ .

6.   She was _____ injured in the car crash.

7.   He didn't study at all so it was no surprise when he _____ the test.

8.   During the Vietnam War, some young men went to Canada to _____ the draft.

9.   A 28-foot sailboat is the perfect size for a one-week _____ .

10.   The union made an _____ attempt to pressure the management, but it finally voted for a new contract.

E. *Vocabulary 2:* **Fill in the blanks with the correct word form.**

1. **(offend)** The umpire rightly took _____ at the player's foul language.

2. **(deter)** A well-trained watchdog is an effective

    _____ against burglars.

3. **(notorious)** The author gained his greatest _____ with his scandalous book about the President's wife.

4. **(congestion)** It took him 45 minutes to cross town because of the

    _____ roads.

5. **(renew)** The magazine offered a special rate for

    _____ a subscription.

F. *Vocabulary 3:* **Write your own sentence using the italicized phrase.**

1. The inspector *advised her to* return after a week and try again.
2. The drivers keep doing it because they never get punished *on the spot.*
3. The other 96 percent *make do* on overloaded buses and trams.
4. A confident young man squealed to a stop, propelled his Fiat backward in a cloud of dust, and *wound up* perpendicular to the white line.

G. *Vocabulary 4:* **These words are often misused. Choose the correct word and explain your choice.**

1. They must also identify traffic symbols from a plastic-covered chart, held upside down when this reporter (**took, passed**) the test.
2. Cairo's population exceeds 8 (**million, millions, millions of**) people.
3. But drivers are not tested on how to behave and there are (**few, a few**) deterrents to recklessness.
4. Applicants must perform (**a, Ø**) series of turns.
5. New York and Cairo are roughly, (**Ø, a, the, as**) same size in population.

RETELL THE STORY

Use the outline below as a guide to retell the story in class.

- the scene at the traffic department office
- the requirements for a driver's license (then versus now)
- the health and vision test
- driving behavior in Cairo
- policemen's attempts to control traffic

- cars versus people
- the rate of traffic accidents

SPEAK UP

1. ONE-MINUTE SPEECH: Give detailed directions on how to get to your house from school by car, by public transportation, or on foot.
2. ROLE PLAY: *Gas Station Attendant and Car Owner.* What do you say when you pull into a gas station?

    Car Owner:
    Ask for gas and have the oil, tires, and radiator checked. Get your windshield cleaned. Complain about how the car is running. Then ask for directions.

    Gas Station Attendant:
    Give advice on repairing the car. Then give directions. Use the expressions below.

    EXPRESSIONS

    Fill'er up, please.
    Would you mind checking the _____ ?
    Could you take a look under the hood?
    It's been stalling (or overheating).
    What's the best way to _____ ?

3. IDENTIFY THESE PARTS OF A CAR: accelerator, brake, clutch, transmission, steering wheel, gear shift, horn, hood, trunk, spare tire, jack, hubcap, speedometer, battery, taillight, headlight, ignition, bumper, fender, rear-view mirror.
4. DESCRIBE THE FOLLOWING DRIVERS: a backseat driver, a reckless driver, a tailgater, an absent-minded driver, a Sunday driver.
5. LISTENING ACTIVITY: Listen to the radio news traffic report at rush hour. Report to the class on the situation.

TABLE 2-1 Car Ownership in the United States

84 percent of all households own at least one car.

33 percent of all households own two cars.

20 percent of all households own three or more cars.

53 percent of college students either own their own cars or are the principal car drivers in their family.

Refer to Table 2-1 in answering the following questions.

1. How do these statistics compare with car ownership in your country?
2. Is a car considered a "necessity" in your country?

TABLE 2-2 Car Ownership and Casualty Rates in Selected Countries

	VEHICLES PER 1,000 POPULATION	CASUALTY RATES PER 100 MILLION VEHICLE-KILOMETERS	
		INJURIES	DEATHS
United States	541	113	2.1
Canada	423	109	2.9
New Zealand	415	87	3.8
Australia	402	82	3.1
West Germany	377	144	3.8
France	355	123	4.6
Italy	308	86	3.3
Finland	271	32	2.0
Denmark	246	57	2.6
Japan	202	153	2.2

Refer to Table 2-2 in answering the following questons.

1. According to the chart, which country has the safest drivers?
2. Which country has the highest fatality rate from automobile accidents?

Refer to the cartoon in answering to the following question:

1. How would a car owner and a taxi driver react in a car accident in your country? What would they say?

"Touché."

TEST YOUR LISTENING COMPREHENSION

A.   Listen to the tape before continuing on. (The Listening Transcript begins on page 129.) Based on the listening, answer the following questions.

1. According to the government report, how many highway deaths involved intoxicated drivers?
2. What proportion of drivers are drunk on weekend nights?
3. What does the government propose to do?
4. What was the Manhattan man charged with?
5. Who was injured?
6. Who was killed?
7. How is the traffic moving on the Long Island Expressway?
8. Why is traffic moving slowly in the Holland Tunnel?
9. What happened to the commuter bus on the George Washington Bridge?
10. Will you get stuck in traffic in the Lincoln Tunnel?

B.   Listen to the newscast again for these words. Can you guess their meaning from the context?

hazards	manslaughter	bumper to bumper
intoxicated	collision	standstill
strengthen laws	tie-ups	stalled
charged with	overturned vehicle	getting stuck

C.   *Listening Carefully:* Your teacher will read aloud the following passage. Fill in the blanks with the missing words.

A government task force _____ a report on the hazards of
(1)

drunk driving. _____ report, half of the 50,000 highway
(2)

_____ last year involved intoxicated drivers. Annually, drunk
(3)

drivers cause 80,000 _____ , 750,000 serious injuries, and 5
(4)

_____ dollars in economic _____ . Federal studies
(5)   (6)

show that on weekend nights _____ ten motorists is intoxicated
(7)

but just _____ 2,000 is arrested. The _____ proposed
(8)   (9)

to _____ laws against drunk driving.
(10)

INTERVIEW _____

Use these questions as a guide to interview a classmate. Add questions of your own.

1. How do you get a driver's license in your country? How much does it cost? Is accident insurance mandatory?

2. Are traffic laws strictly enforced? For example, what happens to a driver in your country who double-parks, speeds, blows the horn, goes through a red light, parks on a sidewalk, doesn't use a turn signal, doesn't use seat belts, or hits a pedestrian? (fined, arrested, license suspended, license revoked)

3. If you are caught driving a car without a license, what will happen?

4. If you are caught driving while intoxicated, what will happen?

5. How do driving habits in the United States compare with driving habits in your country? (politeness, speed, safety)

 6. Have you had a personal experience in the United States while driving a car to illustrate how American drivers act? Describe it.

3 *Worthy of Contempt*

Racial prejudice can be as brutal as a lynching or as subtle as the use of a first name. The author of this article believes that even subtle racial discrimination has no place in the courtroom, no matter what crime a person is charged with. Here is the story of a civil rights lawyer who ended up in jail because he insisted that a judge treat his client with respect.

WORTHY OF CONTEMPT

By TOM WICKER

In the *New York Times* roundup of Supreme Court decisions, the story made one paragraph: "The court also declined to hear an appeal by Millard C. Farmer . . . from two convictions for criminal contempt of court. . . . Mr. Farmer had accused the judge of 'covering up' racism in the courtroom."

The rest of the story needs to be told. It began in 1974 when a black man named George Street took his 16-year-old common-law wife to the hospital in Blackshear, Georgia to deliver a baby. The hospital demanded more advance payment than Mr. Street could make. In a taxi he drove around town trying to borrow the money; when he had run up a $30 cab fare, the driver demanded payment and brandished a blackjack. George Street stabbed and killed him.

He was convicted and sentenced to death. But on appeal, the Supreme Court ruled that his jurors had not been properly questioned about their views on capital punishment. The Court ordered the case returned to Pierce County Superior Court, not for retrial but solely to determine before another jury whether the death penalty had been properly imposed.

Millard Farmer, a civil rights lawyer who heads a group called Team Defense, at that point entered the case as counsel for George Street. In seven weeks of rigorous selection, Mr. Farmer put together a jury of ten blacks and two whites, although Pierce County is only 16 percent black. Ultimately, it took only 20 minutes to sentence George Street to life imprisonment instead of electrocution.

Mr. Farmer and Team Defense operate on the theory that the criminal justice system in the South is heavily tainted with racism both latent and overt. Their tactic is to challenge that racism frontally. In the George Street case, as a consequence, Mr. Farmer was sentenced to a total of four days in jail for instances of what Judge Elie Holton called contempt of court.

One such instance occurred when George Street took the stand and the prosecutor, M. C. Pritchett, consistently referred to him by his first name. As a tape recording demonstrates, Mr. Farmer politely objected that his client should be called "mister" like any other witness. Judge Holton declined to so order and Mr. Farmer responded:

"Your honor . . . it's a mean thing for you to call black people by their first name and to call white people 'mister.' We're not going to have a double standard, we're not going to be a part of it, and we're not going to have it."

Judge Holton:	"Objection overruled."
Mr. Farmer:	"Your honor, it's a form of discrimination . . ."
Judge Holton:	"Objection's overruled."
Prosecutor:	"George . . ."

Mr. Farmer:	"Your honor, I object again to his calling my client George ... He's used the term 'colored folks' ... all of those things are racial slurs. This prosecutor is a racist. And we've got to prevent it from coming through to the jury ... That's got to stop ... if black people are to have equal justice, and it can't stop if objection is not made to it at the proper time."
Judge Holton:	"Objection overruled."
Prosecutor:	"George ..."
Mr. Farmer:	"Your honor, I object."
Judge Holton:	"Mr. Sheriff, sit this gentleman down by the name of Mr. Farmer. Don't make that objection again. I'm going to let you have it as a continuing objection throughout the trial."

80

85

90

95

100

A colloquy followed in which the judge refused to let Mr. Farmer argue further, offer a motion, introduce evidence, or even confer with his client.

105

Mr. Farmer:	"Your honor, do you object to me calling you Elie?"
Judge:	"Mr. Farmer, do not ask the court any such question as that. That is a direct confront of the court ... If you do that again, I will consider it as a contempt of this court."
Mr. Farmer:	"When may I make an objection?"
Judge:	"Are you going to allow procedure of cross-examination of this witness?"

110

115

Mr. Farmer:	"Your honor, I feel like in representing my client ..."	
Judge:	"Mr. Farmer, this court finds your continual interruption ... to be in contempt of court ... It is the judgment of this court that you be sentenced to the common jail of this county for a period of 24 hours. Mr. Sheriff, take Mr. Farmer away."	120 125

Mr. Farmer was taken to the county jail, put in a cell with George Street, but was soon released on bond. He sought in vain to have the Street case removed to federal court, but a federal judge worked out an informal arrangement with Judge Holton and Prosecutor Pritchett that during the rest of the trial George Street would not be referred to by any name at all.

130

135

Now the Supreme Court has refused even to hear Millard Farmer's appeal of his sentences for such "contempt." Soon he will have to start serving his total of four days in the common jail of Pierce County. And of other lawyers in his state, he might well be asking Thoreau's famous question: "Why are you not here?"*

140

145

*Henry David Thoreau (1817–1862) was an American writer and philosopher whose most famous essay was "On Civil Disobedience." His famous question came in response to a friend who came to visit him in jail after Thoreau had been arrested for refusing to pay taxes to support the Mexican-American War. The concept of civil disobedience as expressed by Thoreau has influenced such great leaders as Gandhi and Martin Luther King.

TEST YOUR READING COMPREHENSION

A. Based on the reading, decide whether the following statements are true or false.

1. The author holds Judge Holton in contempt.
2. Millard Farmer wanted the prosecutor to call his client "Mr. George."
3. The Supreme Court gave George Street another chance to prove that he didn't kill the taxi driver.
4. Judge Holton didn't mind if Mr. Farmer called him "Elie."
5. Mr. Farmer won the case he handled for Mr. Street.
6. The author believes the Supreme Court should have reversed Mr. Farmer's conviction because all lawyers should challenge racial discrimination in the courtroom.
7. The prosecutor calls all witnesses by their first names.
8. The hospital in Blackshear, Georgia, wouldn't admit Mr. Street's wife only because she was black.
9. The author feels that lawyers should obey judges in the courtroom.

B. Which of the sentences above best states the main idea of the reading? Circle it.

C. *Vocabulary in Context:* **Without using a dictionary, study how the following words or phrases are used in the reading. Work together in pairs to figure out what the words mean.**

(7) covering up
(19) brandished
(69) a double standard
(72) objection overruled
(101) a colloquy

D. *Vocabulary 1:* **Fill in the blanks with the correct word.**

appeal	contempt of court	life imprisonment	slur
bond	cross-examination	take the stand	overt
common-law	latent	sentenced	overruled

1. The defendant was freed on $5,000 _____ .

2. "One more outburst and I will hold you in _____ ."

3. After the jury found the defendant guilty of murder, the judge _____ him to _____ .

4. The judge told the witness to _____ .

5. Discrimination against blacks in housing today is more _____ than _____ .

6. The conviction was overturned on _____ .

7. The prosecutor's objection was _____ and the _____ of the witness continued.

8. After living together for ten years, she became his _____ wife.

9. Because of the racial _____ , the passenger filed a complaint with the taxi commission.

E. *Vocabulary 2:* Fill in the blanks with the correct word form.

1. (die)   He has been _____ for over a year.

2. (prosecute)   The informer made a deal with the _____ attorney.

3. (worthy)   He decided the price wasn't _____ the aggravation.

4. (race)   The black prizefighter called South Africa a _____ country and refused to defend his title there.

5. (evidence)   What has to be done is _____ .

6. (confront)   When _____ with the evidence, he confessed his part in the crime.

7. (convict)   Nothing I could say would alter his _____ that the election was a fraud.

F. *Vocabulary 3:* Write your own sentence using the italicized phrase.

1. When he had *run up* a $30 cab fare, the driver demanded payment and brandished a blackjack.
2. "... it's a mean thing for you to call black people by their first name and to call white people 'mister.' We're not going to have *a double standard.*"
3. "I *object to his* call*ing* my client George."
4. "This prosecutor is a racist. And we've got to *prevent* it *from* com*ing* through to the jury."
5. He sought *in vain* to have the Street case removed to federal court.
6. "... Mr. Farmer had *accused* the judge *of* 'cover*ing* up' racism in the courtroom."

G. *Vocabulary 4:* **These words are often misused. Choose the correct word and explain your choice.**

1. In a taxi he drove around town trying to (**lend, borrow**) money.
2. He was convicted and sentenced to (**death, dead, died**).
3. George Street took his (**16-years-old, 16-year-old**) common-law wife to the hospital at Blackshear, Georgia.
4. The judge refused to let Mr. Farmer (**to argue, argue, arguing**) further, offer a motion, introduce (**a, an, 0**) evidence, or even confer with his client.
5. And of (**another, other, others**) lawyers in his state, he might well be asking Thoreau's famous question: "Why are you not here?"

RETELL THE STORY

Use the outline below as a guide to retell the story in class.

- George Street's crime and conviction
- Mr. Street's appeal to the Supreme Court
- Millard Farmer's defense of George Street
- Mr. Farmer's reason for objecting
- Judge Holton's ruling
- Mr. Farmer's appeal to the Supreme Court
- Mr. Farmer's punishment
- Thoreau's famous question

SPEAK UP

1. ONE-MINUTE SPEECH: Choose either of these topics.
   A. Briefly describe how the court system works in your country. Is every defendant entitled to a free lawyer? Is the accused innocent until proven guilty? How many judges normally hear a case? Is there a jury system? Can the accused be held in jail without charges being brought up against him? Is there a right of appeal to a higher court? Are trials open to the public? Are judges appointed or elected?
   B. Report on a crime and a trial from the newspapers. Concisely state the facts of the crime and the outcome of the trial.
2. ROLE PLAY: Reenact George Street's trial for murder. Choose a judge, a prosecutor, a defendant, a defense attorney, and witnesses. The rest of the class members will be the jury. The jury will decide whether he is guilty or not guilty. The judge will decide on the punishment.
3. DEBATE: Should capital punishment be abolished? Here are some points for and against the proposition. Think of other reasons besides these to support your position. The class should take a vote at the conclusion of the debate. Use the expressions listed at the end.

PRO	CON
1. Capital punishment does not deter crime.	1. The threat of capital punishment deters crime.
2. It is unfairly applied; most prisoners on death row are poor and black.	2. The Bible says, "An eye for an eye, a tooth for a tooth."
3. There is always the possibility that someone will be executed for a crime he or she did not commit.	3. It's too expensive to keep murderers in jail all their lives.
4. Even if rehabilitation is impossible, society can protect itself by imposing a life sentence.	4. Some prisoners will never be rehabilitated and should be executed before they kill again.

EXPRESSIONS

I'm afraid I don't get your point.
What are you trying to say?
What you are really saying is . . . .
Do you really believe that . . . ?
Well, I think you're mistaken.
Actually, . . .
In fact, . . .
The truth is . . . .

4. RESEARCH: Find out more about Henry David Thoreau. Go to the library and prepare a short presentation on his life and his beliefs.

TABLE 3-1   Some Countries Without the Death Penalty

Austria	Denmark	Iceland	Sweden
Belgium	Dominican Republic	India	Switzerland
Bolivia	Ecuador	Italy	United Kingdom
Brazil	Finland	Panama	Uruguay
Canada	France	Portugal	Venezuela
Costa Rica	Honduras	Spain	West Germany

Refer to Table 3-1 in answering the following questions.

1. Has your native country abolished the death penalty? If so, when? What do you think influenced your country to abolish capital punishment? If not, have there been attempts to change the laws providing for executions?

2. Which groups or parties in your country favor the death penalty? Which oppose it?

TABLE 3-2 How Prejudiced Are White Americans?

84% would vote for a qualified black for president.

93% believe that blacks have the right to live anywhere.

28% would favor a law prohibiting interracial marriages.

4.5% would object to sending their children to a school where a few of the children are black.

11% would object strongly if a family member wanted to bring a black friend home to dinner.

After looking at Table 3-2, answer the following questions.

1. From what you know about the United States, how accurate do these figures seem to you? Why?
2. How would you have responded to this survey?
3. How would most people in your native country respond?

TEST YOUR LISTENING COMPREHENSION _____

A. Listen to the tape before continuing on. (The Listening Transcript appears on page 130.) Based on the listening, answer the following questions.

1. Did the black couple win their suit against the landlord?
2. What made Mr. Williams go to court?
3. What is the landlord's attorney going to do?
4. Why have people gathered in Memphis, Tennessee?
5. Who was Dr. King?
6. What happened on April 4, 1968?
7. Why was King in Memphis in 1968?

B. Listen to the newscast again for these words. Can you guess their meaning from the context?

granted a judgment
award
testimony
deliberated
reaching its verdict
an appeal
the late
commemorate
striking

C. *Listening Carefully.* Your teacher will read aloud the following passage. Fill in the blanks with the missing words.

In the top story today, a black couple _____ a judgment for
                                              (1)

$30,000 _____ a landlord in Westchester, New York,
              (2)

_____ award ever _____ housing discrimination case.
      (3)   (4)
Mr. Thorton Williams, a computer programmer for IBM, began looking

_____ apartment in Westchester after his company transferred
      (5)

him from Chicago. According to the testimony _____ trial, Mr.
                                                      (6)

Williams and his wife visited two buildings in White Plains _____
                                                                    (7)

defendant, Richard Wexler. Although both apartments displayed "Apart-

ment for Rent'' signs, the Williams family _____ Mr. Wexler that
                                                    (8)

the   apartments   _____   rented.   Then   they   brought
                              (9)

_____ in federal court under the Fair Housing Act that prohibits
      (10)

discrimination _____ or rental of housing.
                        (11)

INTERVIEW

Use these questions as a guide to interview a classmate. Add questions of your own.

1. Is any group in your country discriminated against for any of the following reasons: race, religion, language, nationality, sex, occupation, region, etc? Briefly describe the history of these people.

2. In what ways are these people discriminated against? (jobs, housing, education, religious freedom, justice system)

3. Is marriage with a member of this group frowned upon? Give an example of what would happen.

4. Does the government have programs designed to reduce this prejudice? Does the government itself discriminate?

5. Are national attitudes toward this group changing? If so, why and how?

6. Is this group in any way organized to fight against discrimination? Is there anyone helping in this fight? Describe the situation in detail.

7. Thoreau believed in civil disobedience. How important do you think an individual's conscience is? Has anyone practiced civil disobedience in your country? If so, what happened? Would you ever consider not obeying a law you believed was unjust? Explain.

8. Would you have found George Street guilty or not guilty of murder if you had been on the jury? If you had found him guilty, what sentence would you have imposed?

9. Do you think Mr. Farmer was guilty of contempt of court? Why or why not?

4 Burned-Up Bosses Snuff Out Prospects of Jobs for Smokers

"Does anyone mind if I smoke?"

The image of a smoker in the United States used to be that of a tall, rugged, handsome cowboy who radiated health and confidence. However, since the Surgeon General now requires all cigarette packages and advertising to carry health warnings, the image of a smoker has changed drastically. The following article describes this new attitude toward workers who smoke.

BURNED-UP BOSSES SNUFF OUT PROSPECTS OF JOBS FOR SMOKERS

DOES A PACK OF CIGARETTES MEAN 20 BREAKS IN A WORKDAY?

By JENNIFER BINGHAM HULL

Smokers have learned a lot about humility in recent years. Relegated to the rear of airplanes or the drafty section of restaurants, they are some-
5 times even unable to rent the apartment of their choice. Now smokers face a new form of discrimination: Smoking, it seems, may be hazardous to the chances of getting a job.
10 Citing everything from health hazards and productivity losses to outright stupidity as reasons, some employers are resolutely closing the door to job seekers who smoke.
15 Others will hire smokers but forbid them to smoke in the workplace. Both practices appear to be perfectly legal.
"We have two professional part-time project consultants who will
20 never be brought on full-time because of their heavy smoking"; says Matthew Levine, the president of Pacific Select Corp., a sports marketing firm in San Francisco. Mr. Levine explains
25 he won't hire the offenders because they would irritate those who work long hours in close quarters with them. And they would frustrate his efforts to maintain a "clean, fresh
30 atmosphere" in Pacific's handsome new offices.
Job candidates at Seattle-based Radar Electric Inc. find the question "Do you smoke?" written in red at
35 the top of the application form. Those who answer "yes" are told they needn't bother filling out the rest of the form. There won't be any job for them at Radar. Several hundred confessed smokers have been turned 40 away since Radar President Warren McPherson started the policy five years ago. He defends his stance by quoting a private survey that showed that nonsmoking employees of the 45 electrical-equipment maker were more productive than those who smoked.

Less Productive?

Employers who shun smokers 50 usually echo Mr. McPherson's complaint that smokers are less productive than nonsmokers. They argue that people use cigarettes as a break from work, so smoking a pack of ciga- 55 rettes on the job could mean 20 breaks a day. Smoking-related illness can also cause high absenteeism, says the National Center for Health Statistics, which estimates that sick smok- 60 ers cost businesses $25.8 billion in lost productivity in 1980.
The Tobacco Institute, a Washington-based group of U.S. cigarette makers, disputes such conclusions. It 65 points to other studies that show that depriving smokers of the opportunity to indulge can impair their productiv-

ity. "We all have our little things we do at work which others say waste time," says a spokesman.

A spot check of 15 employment agencies around the country indicates that hostility toward smokers is building in executive offices. Increasingly, managers are requesting that agencies send them nonsmokers. Such requests had best be heeded, notes E. Eileen Nock at Manpower Inc. in Milwaukee, gazing at an unpaid bill on her desk. A client balked at honoring it when the nonsmoking temporary he ordered from Manpower turned out to have the habit.

Some employers who don't like smoking on the job worry that a policy of turning away applicants who smoke might be discriminatory. They solve their dilemma by prohibiting smoking on company premises.

Isn't it illegal to discriminate against smokers? No, says the federal Equal Employment Opportunity Commission—unless the result is discrimination on the basis of national origin, race, religion, sex, or age. If, for example, an employer hired men who smoked but not women, there could be a problem, says an EEOC spokesman.

Sheepish Smokers

Smokers, no doubt cowed by official warnings that they could be puffing disease down the throats of their neighbors, by and large meekly submit to no-smoking-on-the-job rules. They ask only to be left to puff in peace off the job.

Coffee breaks are "my time," says Virginia Meyers, the president of Bright Futures Agency, an employment service in Los Angeles. Mrs. Meyers adds that she wouldn't hesitate to complain to job-discrimination authorities if an employer refused to hire her after she agreed not to smoke in the office.

In some cases, the refusal to hire smokers has more to do with appearances than output. Marianne Gentille, an administrative assistant in the Oak Brook, Ill. office of Peat, Marwick, Mitchell & Co., makes a point of hiring a nonsmoking receptionist, although she smokes. "It's always more impressive to meet a person who doesn't smell like smoke or have a cigarette hanging out of her mouth," Mrs. Gentille says. Like many managers, Mrs. Gentille is willing to hire some smokers if their job responsibilities keep them out of public sight.

But some smoking habits get employers so burned up they decide to ban all smokers from the company. Driving up to his headquarters with an important client and finding the flower beds full of cigarette ends and an employee smoking in the doorway was too much for Pro-Tec Inc. President Dennis Burns. Pro-Tec Inc., a West Coast marketer of protective athletic equipment, won't hire smokers anymore. Doesn't Mr. Burns worry he might be passing up talent by turning away smokers? "How smart can they be with all the evidence of what smoking does to your health?" he asks.

Retorts Frank Farrell, the executive vice-president of a Manhattan smokers' rights group called Smokers United: "Who the hell can say smoking dulls the mind when most of the wizards in chess and bridge that I know smoke like fiends?"

Other employers, while remaining firm on a policy of no smoking on the job, sympathize with smokers and try to help them break the habit. At Cybertek Computer Products Inc. in Los Angeles, employees who quit smoking get a $500 bonus.

TEST YOUR READING COMPREHENSION

A.   Based on the reading, decide whether the following statements are true or false.

1. Smoking in private offices is prohibited by law.
2. An increasing number of employers believe nonsmokers make more productive workers.
3. Some companies allow workers to smoke only on their coffee breaks.
4. Smokers are absent from work more often than nonsmokers.
5. The Tobacco Institute says that smoking on the job can improve the productivity of workers who smoke.
6. It's illegal to discriminate against men and women who smoke.
7. Employees at Cybertek Computer Products pay a $500 fine if they are caught smoking.
8. We can tell from the article that the author is a nonsmoker.

B.   Which of the sentences above best states the main idea of the reading? Circle it.

C.   *Vocabulary in Context:* Without using a dictionary, study how the following words or phrases are used in the reading. Work together in pairs to figure out what the words mean.

(50) shun
(51) echo
(78) heeded
(80) gazing
(102) cowed
(134) burned up
(155) fiends

D.   *Vocabulary 1:* Fill in the blanks with the correct word.

balk	drafty	resolutely	submit
ban	puffing	retort	
deprive	relegated	sheepish	

1. Her lack of education _____ her to low-paying jobs.

2. The soldiers _____ refused to surrender.

3. David looked _____ when his teacher asked him to explain his absence.

4. Close the window! It's _____ in here.

5. Even I would _____ at paying that price for a simple pair of pants.

6. He ran so fast to catch the train that he was still _____ when

the conductor asked him for his ticket.

7. The police had no choice but to _____ further demonstrations after the last outbreak of violence.

8. The reporter's rude question deserved a quick _____ .

9. Gina was never the type who would _____ to strict discipline.

10. It wasn't fair to _____ the boy of a new bicycle at Christmas.

E. *Vocabulary 2:* Fill in the blanks with the correct word form.

1. **(choice)**   Have you _____ what course you want to take?

2. **(irritate)**   Please turn off that _____ music.

3. **(discriminate)**   The hiring policy was _____ against older people.

4. **(impress)**   He made an _____ speech on behalf of the company.

5. **(indulge)**   He had an _____ mother who jumped whenever he cried.

6. **(impair)**   His sight was seriously _____ after the accident.

7. **(hostile)**   We felt his _____ when he glared at us.

8. **(product)**   She was the most _____ worker he had ever had.

9. **(offend)**   Because this was his third _____ this year, the judge sentenced him to jail.

10. **(absent)**   He had to repeat the eleventh grade because of excessive _____ .

F. *Vocabulary 3:* Write your own sentence using the italicized phrase.

1. Others will hire smokers but *forbid them to* smoke in the workplace.
2. Isn't it illegal to *discriminate against* smokers?
3. *A spot check* of 15 employment agencies around the country indicates that hostility toward smokers is building in executive offices.
4. Some employers worry that a policy of *turning away* applicants who smoke might be discriminatory.
5. They solve their dilemma by *prohibiting* smoking on company premises.
6. Other employers *sympathize with* smokers.

7. Doesn't he worry that he might be *passing up* talent by turning away smokers?

G. *Vocabulary 4:* These words are often confused. Choose the correct word and explain your choice.

1. Smoking, it seems, (**maybe, may be**) hazardous to the chances of getting a job.
2. Sick smokers cost businesses $25.8 (**billions, billion**) in lost productivity in 1980.
3. Employees who quit (**to smoke, smoking**) get a $500 bonus.
4. "It's always more impressive to meet a person who doesn't smell (**as, like**) smoke."
5. A West Coast marketer of protective athletic (**equipment, equipments**) won't hire smokers anymore.

RETELL THE STORY

Use the outline below as a guide to tell the story in class.

- the change in employer attitudes toward smokers
- the part-time consultants who smoke
- "Do you smoke?" on job applications
- smoking and illness
- Tobacco Institute on productivity
- employment agencies and smoking
- is it discrimination?
- sheepish smokers
- smoking and appearance
- smoking and stupidity
- incentive to stop smoking

SPEAK UP

1. ONE-MINUTE SPEECH: Kicked the habit? Explain to the class how you did it. Got the habit? Explain how you started smoking. Never smoked? Describe the image of a smoker in your country.
2. ROLE PLAY: *Smoker and Nonsmoker.* You are sitting in a restaurant and there is a smoker sitting at the table next to you. Ask him or her to stop smoking. Ask politely at first, but when the smoker continues, be more insistent. Use the expressions below.

FOR THE NONSMOKER

Would you mind putting out your cigarette?
Could you please stop smoking?
I'd really appreciate it if you would stop.

The smoke is bothering me.

FOR THE SMOKER

Is my cigarette bothering you?
Oh, I'll be through soon.
I'm almost finished.
Oh, I'm so sorry! (terribly sorry, awfully sorry)

3.   DEBATE: Should tobacco smoking be banned?

PRO	CON
1. Smoking is addictive.	1. People smoke because it's relaxing and enjoyable. They can quit when they want to.
2. Smoking causes cancer.	
3. Smoking pollutes the air for nonsmokers.	2. The evidence linking tobacco and cancer is inconclusive.
4. It's a waste of money.	
5. The land used to grow tobacco should be used to grow food.	3. Smoking can be restricted to well-ventilated areas.
	4. People have the right to spend their money as they see fit.
	5. If tobacco were banned, people would grow it illegally.

TABLE 4-1   Fact Sheet on Smoking

54 million Americans smoke.
75 percent started before they were 21.
The average American smoker buys a pack and a half of cigarettes a day.
34 million Americans have quit smoking.
A cigarette smoker is 10 times more likely to die of lung cancer than a nonsmoker.
122,000 Americans will die of lung cancer this year.

Refer to Table 4-1 in answering the following question.

1.   How can these figures be used to support the proposition, "Smoking is addictive"? How can they be used to refute it?

TEST YOUR LISTENING COMPREHENSION

A.   Listen to the tape before continuing on. (The Listening Transcript appears on page 131.) Based on the listening, answer the following questions.

1.   What is Proposition 10?
2.   What happened two years ago to a similar proposition?

"Thank you for not smoking."

3. If Proposition 10 passed, what would happen to violators?
4. What did the report in the New England Journal of Medicine say?
5. What event is being planned by the American Cancer Society for next Thursday?
6. What are the police and fire departments planning to do in Sarasota, Florida?

B. Listen to the newscast again for these words. Can you guess their meaning from the context?

go to the polls
violators
fined
rejected
second-hand smoke
lung damage
light up

C. *Listening Carefully:* Your teacher will read aloud the following passage. Fill in the blanks with the missing words.

Voters in California will go _____ next week to vote on Prop-
                                        (1)

osition 10, a proposal to require no-smoking areas _____ public
                                                              (2)

places. Proposition 10 _____ require employers to establish no-
                              (3)

smoking areas _____ employees requested it. Violators of the
                      (4)

proposed law _____ $15.00. A similar proposition
                      (5)

_____ two years ago after tobacco companies _____
        (6)   (7)

$6.3 million _____ advertising campaign _____ .
                    (8)   (9)

INTERVIEW

> Use these questions as a guide to interview a classmate. Add questions of your own.
>
> 1. How old do you have to be to buy cigarettes in your country?
> 2. Do women smoke?
> 3. How are people encouraged or discouraged from smoking in your country?
> 4. Is it considered impolite to smoke in front of teachers, elders, parents, or bosses?
> 5. Should smoking be banned in any of the following places: offices, elevators, schools, stores, airplanes, buses, subways, restaurants, or theaters? Why or why not?
> 6. Tobacco companies argue that prohibiting a person from smoking where he or she wants to is an affront to one's personal freedom. What is your opinion?
> 7. If somebody's smoke were bothering you, what would you do? If someone told you that your cigarette was bothering him, what would you do?
> 8. Cigarette ads are prohibited on American television. Should all cigarette advertising be banned?
> 9. All cigarette packages in the United States must bear a health warning. Do you think there should be a warning on cigarette packages? What are some other ideas on how people can be discouraged from smoking?

5

The Experts on Product Safety: What They Say and What They Do

Melinda Levine

One of the results of the consumer movement in America in the 1960's and 1970's was the increasing role of government in protecting people from dangerous products. Ralph Nader's book on the hazards of defective automobiles, Unsafe at Any Speed, *and the movement he helped create, led to the passage of many new consumer protection laws. One of those laws created the Consumer Product Safety Commission, whose job it is to protect Americans from hazardous products. However, not even the most dedicated consumer protection advocate can escape all the dangerous products now on the market, as is demonstrated by the following article.*

THE EXPERTS ON PRODUCT SAFETY: WHAT THEY SAY AND WHAT THEY DO

By MICHAEL DECOURCY HINDS

WASHINGTON—June 3—The five members of the Consumer Product Safety Commission do not always practice what they preach.

5 Some of their offices have defective chrome chairs in which visitors' feet become entangled. None of their bathrooms or kitchens has an electrocution-preventing "ground fault
10 interceptor," a device that, as commissioners, they officially recommend for home wiring. And two of them will not give up defective coffee pots that were recalled two years
15 ago.

One of the last is Sam Zagoria, an avid promotor of the agency's responsibility to monitor product recalls. He still has two of the 18 million pots that
20 were recalled by the company because their plastic handles tended to fall off and a number of people had been scalded while pouring coffee.

The pot makes good coffee, Mr.
25 Zagoria says, adding: "My wife, Sylvia, knows there is a potential problem, so she uses the pot on the counter or over the sink."

"The point of a recall," he contin-
30 ued, "is to alert people to a potential hazard."

More Safety Conscious

None of this is to say that Mr. Zagoria and the four other commis-
35 sioners do not take their roles as private consumers seriously. They do,

checking *Consumer Reports* magazine before making major purchases and complaining loudly when they end up with a lemon. But despite their con-
40 stant dealing with coroners' reports and emergency room statistics that link scores of products with deaths and injuries, none seems to have turned into a paranoid consumer.
45 "I'm no more paranoid than I ever was," said Edith Barksdale Sloan, another member of the panel. "But I'm a lot more safety conscious than I was before coming to the commission."
50 Still, she refuses to give up her Corning coffee pot, which was a wedding gift. "I carry it around with a hot pad and don't permit anyone else to use it," she said.
55 For a very different reason, Mrs. Sloan held onto a pair of her son's pajamas, which were recalled in 1977 when the flame-retardant chemical Tris was identified as a suspected car-
60 cinogen. "Douglas wore those pajamas for a long time, long enough to make me concerned," Mrs. Sloan said. "So I am keeping them as evidence just in case he has problems later on."
65

Chairman's Complaint

The chairman of the agency, Nancy Harvey Steorts, is acutely aware of product hazards. Over the

Continued on Page 42, Column 1

70 Memorial Day weekend she caught her foot in a loose flagstone in her back yard and badly sprained her ankle. "If I knew who built this patio, I would really complain," she said. "The home 75 improvement area is a big problem for consumers."

Before Mrs. Steorts buys any product, she determines what recourse she has if a problem should 80 develop. "I buy for service," she said. If the product doesn't work, she calls the president of the company, without mentioning the commission or her post, to complain. "I usually get 85 through," she said.

But sometimes she doesn't. "I am on a personal campaign against Datsun," Mrs. Steorts says. "I can't tell you how many people I have discour- 90 aged from buying a Datsun because of the way they have treated me."

Mrs. Steorts, pleased with a Datsun 510, traded it in three years ago for a Datsun 810. But, she says, the 95 car gets only 12 miles per gallon, less than half the car's advertised performance. Despite many trips to the shop and many telephone calls to company underlings, she remains a "totally dissatisified customer." 100

A Classic Example

Another commissioner, R. David Pittle, a former professor of Engineering at Carnegie-Mellon University in Pittsburgh, keeps some of the commis- 105 sion's defective chrome-and-wicker chairs in his office as "conversation pieces." The chairs have extended side arms that often catch visitors' legs. "The chair is a classic example of 110 aesthetics winning over safe design," Mr. Pittle said, hastening to add that a former commission chairman had bought them.

Mr. Pittle is a tough customer. 115 "When I go shopping for something," he said, "I try to take the product apart to see how it is put together, how well made it is, and if it can be easily misused." 120

"My wife doesn't like to go shopping with me," he added. "She says I take too long and drive the salesman crazy."

TEST YOUR READING COMPREHENSION

A. Based on the reading, decide whether the following statements are true or false.

1. The five members of the Consumer Product Safety Commission always follow the advice they give others.
2. Members of the Consumer Product Safety Commission consider themselves careful consumers even though they still use products that have been recalled.
3. The commission determined that the coffee pots had defective handles.
4. Working for consumer safety has made Mrs. Sloan afraid to buy anything.
5. A recall warns consumers about a potential danger.
6. Mrs. Sloan is keeping her son's pajamas in case he becomes ill.

7. When Mrs. Steorts has a problem with a product, she calls the president of the company.

8. Mrs. Steorts feels that more people should buy Datsuns.

9. Mr. Pittle keeps the defective chrome-and-wicker chairs because they are comfortable.

10. Mr. Pittle's wife enjoys shopping with her husband.

B. Which of the sentences above best states the main idea of the reading? Circle it.

C. *Vocabulary in Context:* Without using a dictionary, study how the following words or phrases are used in the reading. Work together in pairs to figure out what the words mean.

(4) practice what they preach

(30) alert

(60) Tris

(71) flagstone

(78) what recourse she has

(107) conversation pieces

(111) aesthetics

D. *Vocabulary 1:* Fill in the blanks with the correct word.

acutely	entangled	paranoid	scalded
avid	lemon	potential	underling
coroner	link	recalled	

1. As a social worker, she tried not to get too _____ in her clients' problems.

2. When tests showed that the steering wheel was defective, the company _____ all the cars.

3. He's been an _____ reader since he was given his first book.

4. The pan was so hot that she _____ the milk.

5. Although he's not ready to take over his father's position, he does show great _____ .

6. After her unexpected death, the _____ was asked to perform an autopsy.

7. Her research established a _____ between the deaths of the birds and the use of pesticides.

8. After receiving her first speeding ticket, she became _____ about driving too fast.

9. His experience abroad made him _____ aware of the problems foreigners run up against in a new country.

10. Her new car was always in the repair shop; it was quite a _____ !

11. He wanted to be recognized as more than a mere _____ in the company.

E. *Vocabulary 2:* Fill in the blanks with the correct word form.

1. (defect)   The nuclear power plant was shut down because of a _____ pump.

2. (product)   He felt he was most _____ in the morning.

3. (hazard)   At night those mountain roads are _____ .

4. (safe)   Her child's _____ was her main concern.

5. (conscious)   He regained _____ two days after the car accident.

6. (dissatisfy)   The _____ consumers were lined up at the complaint office.

7. (promotion)   After two years, he will be _____ to a managerial position.

F. *Vocabulary 3:* Write your own sentence using the italicized phrase.

1. And two of them will not *give up* defective coffee pots that were recalled two years ago.
2. None of this is to say that Mr. Zagoria and the four other commissioners do not *take* their roles as private consumers *seriously*.
3. They complain loudly when they *end up with* a lemon.
4. If the product doesn't work, she calls the president of the company. "I usually *get through*," she said.
5. "I can't tell you how many people I have *discouraged from* buying a Datsun because of the way they have treated me."
6. "She says I take too long and *drive* the salesman *crazy*."

G. *Vocabulary 4:* These words are often misused. Choose the correct word and explain your choice.

1. None of their bathrooms or kitchens (**has, have**) an electrocution-preventing "ground fault interceptor."
2. He still has two of the 18 (**million, millions**) pots that were recalled by the company (**because, because of**) their plastic handles tended to (**fell, feel, fall**) off and (**a number, the number**) of people had been scalded while pouring coffee.
3. "I'm no more paranoid (**than, then**) I ever was."

4. "I carry it around with a hot pad and don't (**permit, let**) anyone else to use it."
5. They check *Consumer Reports* magazine before (**to make, make, making**) (**mayor, major**) purchases.
6. "Douglas wore those pajamas for (**a, Ø**) long time."

RETELL THE STORY

Use the outline as a guide to tell the story in class.

- the Consumer Product Safety Commission members don't always practice what they preach (coffee pot story)
- what they do before making a purchase
- the problem with the pajamas
- the loose flagstone
- the Datsun car problem
- the chrome-and-wicker chair
- Mr. Pittle's shopping style

SPEAK UP

1. ONE-MINUTE SPEECH: Most Americans are comparison shoppers. They go to several stores to find the best value for their money before making a major purchase. In addition, many people read publications, such as *Consumer Reports*, that give ratings on a wide variety of goods from peanut butter to used cars. Give the class the results of your comparison shopping for something you plan to buy or have recently bought. Describe the best models on the market, their prices, and their features. Explain the reasons for your choice. Suggestion: Go to the library and see how *Consumer Reports* magazine has rated the product you are interested in.

2. ROLE PLAY: *Unhappy Consumer and Customer Service Representative.* Choose one of the following situations, and use the expressions below.

- Return a malfunctioning product.
- Complain about being shortchanged in a supermarket.
- Complain about being overcharged on a telephone bill or on a credit card bill.

EXPRESSIONS

I want my money back.
It's a lemon.
You must have made a mistake.
It hasn't been working.
You should have given me. . . .

I couldn't have done that.

That couldn't have happened.

It's out of the question.

Refer to the article "Product Recalls" in answering the following questions.

1. How would you find out whether a baby rattle given to you as a gift is defective?
2. Which defect in the cars do you think is the most dangerous?

TEST YOUR LISTENING COMPREHENSION

A. Listen to the tape before continuing on. (The Listening Transcript appears on page 131.) Based on the listening, answer the following questions.

1. What kind of cars is General Motors recalling?
2. Is this the biggest recall on record?
3. How will the car owners learn of the recall?
4. What is wrong with the cars?
5. How many accidents has this defect caused?
6. How much will the repair cost car owners?
7. Why did the Health Research Group write "Pills That Don't Work"?
8. How much money did Americans spend on health care last year?
9. According to Dr. Sidney Wolfe, what is happening to the doctor–patient relationship?

B. Listen to the newscast for these words. Can you guess their meaning from the context?

on record

notification

rear suspension bolts

rear axle

for the better

C. *Listening Carefully:* Your teacher will read aloud the following passage. Fill in the blanks with the missing words.

The General Motors Corporation announced today that it _____ to recall 6.4 million mid-size cars _____
        (1)   (2)

between 1978 and 1981. This is _____ safety recall on record.
                                          (3)

Product recalls

Household products

Montgomery Schoolhouse baby rattles. The toy could become caught in an infant's throat and cause choking and suffocation.

Products: 61,000 Montgomery Schoolhouse baby rattles sold since September 1981. Made of hardwood, some have colored parts and some have clear varnish finish. Some have metal bells enclosed in wood cages. Some were sold in blister packages with the words "Rattle, Heirloom Quality, Hardwood, Childsafe Color" printed on face. Some were sold in plastic bags with paper insert that said "finest Handcrafted Wooden Toys from Vermont" and the name "TT Bell Rattle" or "TT 5 Disc Rattle." Others were sold without packaging.
What to do: Return to retailer or send to Montgomery Schoolhouse Inc., Montgomery, Vt. 05470 for exchange.

Schowanek baby rattles. Toy could become caught in an infant's throat and cause choking and suffocation.

Products: 2900 Schowanek baby rattles imported since 1981. Made of hardwood, they come in the following shapes: duck on a handle (code number 10875/2); dumbbell (number 10875/33); bowling pin (number 10876/17); dumbbell with pieces of wood on shaft (number 10876/3); barbell with 4 wooden rings on shaft (number 10876/26); handle with head and arms (number 10876/8); cylinder with six holes and bell inside (number 10876/19). Code numbers are on packaging, not on rattles themselves.
What to do: Return to retailer for refund or exchange, or return to Schowanek of America, 454 Third Ave., NYC 10016 for refund.

General Electric drip coffeemakers. A fuse may fail to function as intended, if appliance overheats. That could result in damage to counter top or in a fire.

Products: 200,000 GE drip coffeemakers identified as follows: catalog number B1-3382-0 or B1-3385-0 with date code 634 through 717; catalog number B1-3390-0 with date code 704 through 717; catalog number B1- or B2-3387-0 with date code 618 through 822. Catalog numbers are on the bottom of the coffeemaker, the date codes on the metal prongs of the plug.
What to do: Do not use coffeemaker. Call manufacturer toll-free at 1-800-626-2000 day or night to arrange for free replacement.

Cars

1979-1980 Datsun 310 hatchback. In some cars, defective sockets could cause tail and brake lights to fail.

Models: 72,754 Datsun 310 hatchback cars made from July 1979 through July 1980
What to do: Return to dealer for replacement of lamp harness assembly.

1982 Buick Regal. Under some operating conditions, vibration may cause a fuel line to crack at the carburetor and leak fuel, possibly causing a fire.

Models: 1167 1982 Buick Regal cars made from August 20, 1981, through April 5, 1982.
What to do: Return to dealer for installation of improved fuel line.

1983 Chrysler LeBaron, Dodge Aries and 400, and Plymouth Reliant. In some cars, brake line may rub against parking-brake cable, causing break in line and loss of fluid. This could result in partial loss of braking capability.

Models: 1236 1983 Chrysler LeBaron, Dodge Aries and 400, and Plymouth Reliant cars made last August.
What to do: Return to dealer to reroute brake line.

G.M. said that car owners _____ notification to bring
(4)

_____ to G.M. dealers for replacement of two rear suspension
(5)

bolts. If the bolts break, the rear axle _____ from the car and
(6)

cause _____ control. According to G.M., 27 accidents and 22
(7)

_____ have resulted from this defect. The bolts _____
(8)   (9)
without charge to the owners.

INTERVIEW _____

Use these questions as a guide to interview a classmate. Add questions of your own.

1. Is there a consumer movement in your country? Who are the leaders? Are there organized groups of consumers? Are there consumer publications? Are there consumer protection laws and lobbyists?

    What are the goals of the consumer movement in your country? What are its accomplishments?

    What factors have inhibited the growth of the consumer movement?

    If there is no consumer movement in your country, do you believe there should be one?

    What issues would you like to see a consumer movement address in your country?

2. What can you do in your country if you buy a product that malfunctions?

3. Have you ever returned a product in the United States? Explain what happened.

4. Some critics feel that a government should not interfere with big business. They contend that big business will regulate itself and that the government should let business operate without interference. Do you agree with these critics? Cite some specific examples of government regulation to support your opinion.

6 Singapore Fast Food: Try Pig Intestines or Maybe a Big Mac

The author of this article presents a lively contrast between two very different types of fast food restaurants he found in People's Park, Singapore. Like any good journalist, he tries to be objective when reporting the facts to his readers. His vivid writing style uses many words that will be new to you. Even so, read the article straight through the first time without using your dictionary.

SINGAPORE FAST FOOD: TRY PIG INTESTINES OR MAYBE A BIG MAC

A COMPUTERIZED MCDONALD'S CONTRASTS WITH DIN, CHAOS, AND EXOTIC FARE AT STALLS

By BARRY NEWMAN

SINGAPORE—McDonald's came to Singapore a little over a year ago, opening its first store in a new office building on a wide boulevard of tourist
5 hotels. It was the sort of Asian setting where a McDonald's fits in.

A few months later a second McDonald's appeared. It is in People's Park, a chaotic bazaar near the heart
10 of Chinatown where hundreds of hawkers in a complex of stalls shovel out Singapore's celebrated street food. Under a haze of charcoal smoke, People's Park is mobbed, steamy, and
15 redolent, ringing with the noise of crashing dishes, sputtering fat, and bawling waiters. Its customers have a special appetite for entrails.

In McDonald's, a customer hears
20 not Chinese music but a Ray Charles song. Humidity is supplanted by air conditioning, naked light bulbs by fluorescence. Ronald McDonald swims in an "undersea theme" mosaic of
25 pressed plastic that has been imported, with everything down to the floor tiles, from America.

Through America's plate-glass window, flames are visible leaping
30 under the woks of the Min Ho restaurant across an alley, not 30 feet away. A monkey sits on a table outside the open-ended kitchen eating peanuts.

An old man in wide-legged shorts washes dishes in a wooden tub while a 35 youth pulls roasted ducks from a barrel-shaped oven. Baskets of noodles and vegetables are stacked here and there. Eels slither in a tank.

All Very Messy 40

Here, in direct confrontation, are two great philosophies of fast food. One uses the freezer, the computer, and the business school to manufacture a few simple dishes in never a tick 45 longer than 100 seconds. The other relies on the markets of Chinatown, the abacus, and a covey of cousins, aunts, and grandmothers who pass the hours pulling the roots off bean 50 sprouts to create a profusion of complicated dishes in a minute or two. The first is fast for both cook and customer. The second is fast for the customer, but not fast at all for the cook. 55

Seated at a table at the Min Ho is Kong Hong Kee, 31-year-old son of Min Ho's proprietor. He is swaybacked and shirtless and has a boar's tooth on a chain around his neck. With a small 60 knife, he is shaving the tough ends of the mustard greens heaped before him.

"McDonald's is very busy," he says, speaking Cantonese through an interpreter. "They came here for the traffic. But the people who go there are the English-educated ones, those who grab a bun and walk around town with it in their hands. They like neat packages. Over here, it is all very messy."

Mr. Kong closes his eyes and shakes his head when asked if he has ever had a Big Mac. "The smell is very pungent," he says. "I see food arrive over there in large crates and I get shivers down my back. Chinese people like things fresh."

The manager across the alley is Eddie Lim, who is 30 years old and has studied at Hamburger U. in the United States. He wears a starched shirt and a tie with the McDonald's symbol on it.

Radish Cakes and Cockles

"We don't see ourselves as a stall," he says, sipping a Pepsi. "We are a family restaurant. We have better decor, better seating. We give value for money—the best quality you can find. The greatest difference is courtesy. We don't have anybody standing outside stopping people and yelling, 'Big Mac! Big Mac!'"

The clash of these culinary needs is sharp as can be in Singapore, the mecca of fast food, Asian style. Thousands of stalls line the streets and are collected in the hawker centers of this equatorial island state. They offer a palate-boggling cross-cultural potpourri of Indian, Malay, and Chinese smells and flavors, a melange of cardamom and cumin, coconut milk and shrimp paste, soy sauce and rice wine—all laced with hot red chilies.

This is how to make Laksa: Grate coconuts, squeeze out milk; boil shrimp for stock: pound chilies, lemon grass, shallots, turmeric, candlenuts, shrimp paste, and coriander and fry the mixture; add coconut milk, stock; pour into bowls over noodles and bean sprouts; top with fried bean curd, shredded chicken, pounded dry shrimp, egg, cucumber, and cockles: garnish with chili sauce and diced mint. In the stalls, Laksa is made fresh daily. A bowl is served 30 seconds after it's ordered and costs 50 cents.

The day has its rhythm at People's Park. The cadence of cleavers against chopping blocks builds slowly to the frying, the crashing, and the screaming.

McDonald's has rhythm of its own: At 9 A.M. spatulas are sharpened. At 2 P.M. tartar sauce cartridges are sanitized. At 10 P.M. reconstituted onion is mixed.

The McDonald's grill beeps when it's time for the uniformed cook to flip a hamburger. The bun toaster beeps when the buns are done. The "fish-fillet cooking computer" beeps when the fish is finished.

Across the alley at the Min Ho, nothing beeps. Two cooks stand in the fiery heat before six woks, furiously working six orders at once—plunging crabs into boiling oil, ladling chicken stock over steaming greens, pausing only to wipe the sweat off their arms. The menu has everything but the monkey, and that includes flying foxes, which are large, furry bats. "You want it, we cook it," says Kong Hong Kee.

The Min Ho doesn't have a cash register; money is stashed between two stacked bowls. A party of six, Mr. Kong figures, will spend a total of $10 for a meal, not including beer. He isn't effusive about finances, though the Min Ho could well be a gold mine. Rent is low. There are just 10 employees, and half are family. Help is hard to find, but Mr. Kong doesn't mind.

Continued on Page 52, Column 1

"There's always a family member to
160 tide us over."

French Fries 101

McDonald's has six cash registers,
ringing up 4,000 sales a day, and a
staff of 130 with applicants waiting in
165 line. The staff is trained with guides,
manuals, and a set of 22 videotapes.
Employees take written examinations
in such subjects as French fries,
advanced French fries, shakes, and
170 advanced shakes. The pay, to start, is
75 cents an hour, rising to $1.50 an
hour. "Plus we give them free lunch,"
says Mr. Lim, showing a visitor the
staff room. There a young woman is
175 eating a slab of Chinese luncheon
meat and some Malay fried potatoes
from the stalls. She is so embarrassed
she can't speak.

Everyone who works in McDon-
180 ald's knows how to smile. Clair Ngoi
Ming Chew—the public relations
officer—stands waiting for someone to
make a sour face about a soggy bun,
then rushes, smiling, to apologize. The
185 economic development board of Singapore is so impressed it has asked
McDonald's for help in the national
courtesy campaign.

At the Min Ho, the courtesy cam-
190 paign hasn't made much headway.
When a customer sits down, a pot of
tea is slammed in front of him whether
he wants it or not. He pays 15 cents for
that, plus 5 cents for a wet washcloth.

If a small beer is ordered, a large one is 195
likely to be delivered. If a fish is
ordered, the waiter will carry it out by
the tail and wave it before the customer's nose to prove its freshness,
barking all the while at prospective 200
eaters passing by in a voice loud
enough to damage the inner ear.

Pig's-Brain Soup

All this aside, the choice between
McDonald's and the Min Ho comes 205
down to a matter of taste.

Jerry and Jackie Schulman have
flown for 26 hours from Brooklyn,
N.Y., to sit in the People's Park McDonald's eating Big Macs. Wouldn't they 210
like to try some of this city's famous
stall food?

"My wife has a weak stomach,"
says Mr. Schulman.

Mrs. Schulman scowls. "I don't 215
like Chinese food. The smell. I can't
stand to see it prepared."

Over at the Min Ho, T.K. Phua and
Loh Fu Wah are having lunch. Mr.
Phua has a plate of noodles fried with 220
pig's intestines. Mr. Loh has a bowl of
pig's-brain soup.

"Just a piece of meat between
two pieces of bread," says Mr. Phua of
his experience at McDonald's. "Here, 225
try some guts."

Mr. Loh savors a spoonful of pig's
brains. "I've had a hamburger," he
says. "I don't know. If I eat too much
Western food, I get sick." 230

**TEST YOUR READING
COMPREHENSION** _____

A. Based on this reading, decide whether the following statements are true or false.

1. One similarity between McDonald's and Min Ho's is that the customers are served quickly.
2. The stalls offer a wider variety of food than McDonald's.
3. The waiters at the Min Ho restaurant are courteous.

4. Two very different types of fast food are in People's Park; which you prefer is a matter of personal taste.
5. Help is hard to find for McDonald's.
6. People's Park is an unlikely place for a modern computerized restaurant.
7. The Min Ho restaurant is a family operation.
8. Only Westerners eat at the McDonald's in People's Park.
9. The American couple in the story enjoyed trying the different varieties of food in People's Park.
10. You can tell from the article that the author prefers to eat at McDonald's.

B. **Which of the statements above best states the main idea of the reading? Circle it.**

C. *Vocabulary in Context:* **Without using a dictionary, study how the following words or phrases are used in the reading. Work together in pairs to figure out what the words mean.**

(11) hawkers
(13) haze
(39) slither
(77) crates
(142) ladling
(150) stashed
(160) tide us over
(175) a slab
(183) a sour face
(200) barking

D. *Vocabulary 1:* **Fill in the blanks with the correct word.**

grabbed	proprietor	savored	slammed
messy	pungent	scowled	sputtering
mobbed			

1. The ripe cheese had a _____ smell.

2. The thief _____ the woman's purse and ran away.

3. At rush hour all the trains are _____ .

4. The hot frying pan was _____ grease all over the stove.

5. She angrily _____ the door in his face.

6. After her husband died, she became the _____ of the store.

7. The boss _____ whenever an employee came late.

8. She got so tired of her _____ house that she finally hired a maid.

9. The soup was so delicious that he _____ every spoonful.

E. *Vocabulary 2:* Fill in the blanks with the correct word form.

1. (embarrass)   When the teacher called on her, she was too

_____ to speak.

2. (impress)   The young violinist made an _____ debut.

3. (choose)   Members of the tour were given a

_____ of hotels.

4. (confront)   New parents are _____ with many problems.

5. (sanitize)   He didn't want to eat there because the

conditions weren't _____ .

6. (chaos)   It was a _____ day at the office because the computer broke down.

7. (taste)   The sauce was so _____ that he licked his plate.

8. (rely)   He's totally _____ on his parents for financial support.

9. (courtesy)   Outside big cities, people tend to be more

_____ .

10. (air-condition)   She enjoyed going to the movies in the summer because the theaters were always

_____ .

F. *Vocabulary 3:* Write your own sentence using the italicized phrase.

1. It was the sort of Asian setting where a McDonald's *fits in*.
2. The other *relies on* the markets of Chinatown.
3. "I see food arrive over there in large crates and *I get shivers down my back*."
4. "I don't like Chinese food. The smell. I *can't stand* to see it prepared."
5. If a small beer is ordered, a large one is *likely* to be delivered.
6. At the Min Ho, the courtesy campaign hasn't *made much headway*.

G. *Vocabulary 4:* These words are often misused. Choose the correct word and explain your choice.

1. (It's, Its) customers have a special appetite for entrails.
2. (Sat, seated, seating) at a table at the Min Ho is Kong Hong Kee, (31-year-old, 31 year old, 31 years old) son of Min Ho's proprietor.

3. Eddie Lim, who is (**30-year-old, 30 year old, 30 years old**), has studied at Hamburger U. in the United States.

4. The (**clash, crash**) of these culinary needs is sharp as can be in Singapore, mecca of fast food, Asian style.

5. The pay, to start, is 75 cents an hour, (**raising, rising**) to $1.50 an hour.

6. If a fish is ordered, the waiter will carry it out by the tail and wave it before the customer's nose to (**proof, proove, prove**) its freshness.

RETELL THE STORY

Compare and contrast these "two great philosophies of fast food." Use the outline below as a guide to retell the story in class.

MIN HO'S VERSUS MCDONALD'S

- location
- variety of food
- preparation/method of cooking
- ingredients used/spices
- physical description
- sounds
- help/employees
- service/courtesy
- dress
- customer reactions

SPEAK UP

1. ONE-MINUTE SPEECH: Review a restaurant. Tell about the location, the quality of food, the specialties, the portions, the atmosphere, the comfort, and the price. Use the following vocabulary as necessary.

soggy	raw	spicy	efficient
crisp	burnt	hot	reasonable
juicy	sour	salty	moderate
dry	rancid	tasty	overpriced
chewy	sugary	bland	adequate
tender	stale	greasy	skimpy
tough	fresh	heavy	enormous
overcooked	creamy	light	rude

2. ROLE PLAY: Invite a colleague out to lunch. Your colleague will accept or refuse. Use the expressions below.

"Would you like to join me for lunch?"

ACCEPTANCES	REFUSALS
Yes, I'd be pleased to.	Gee, I'm much too busy today.
I'd love to.	I'd love to tomorrow, but today
Yes, I'm starving.	is out.
Sure, where do you have in mind?	Can I take a rain check?
Sure, I'll be ready in a minute.	Thanks, but my schedule is really tight.
	How about next week?
	Sorry, I'm on a diet.

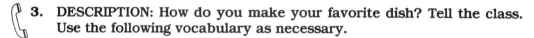

3. **DESCRIPTION:** How do you make your favorite dish? Tell the class. Use the following vocabulary as necessary.

boil	stir fry	stir	dice	a tablespoon of
broil	brown	whip	sprinkle	pour
fry	grate	melt	garnish	top
bake	squeeze	chop	a dash of	add
sauté	peel	slice	a teaspoon of	mix

4. **LISTENING ACTIVITY:** Listen to food or restaurant advertisements on radio and television. Describe an ad to your classmates.

TABLE 6-1   Some Facts About Eating in America

On the average, the dinner meal lasts 20 minutes.
The entire family sits down to dinner together about three times a week.
75 percent of American families eat breakfast together.
32 percent of American families eat dinner while the television set is on.
One-fifth of all Americans are on a diet.

Refer to Table 6-1 in answering the following questions.

1. If the same survey were taken in your country, what do you think the results would be?
2. Which of these facts surprised you? Explain why.

TEST YOUR LISTENING COMPREHENSION

A. Listen to the tape before continuing on. (The Listening Transcript appears on page 132.) Based on the listening, answer the following questions.

1. What meats are Americans eating less of?
2. Why are Americans consuming less whole milk?
3. How much ice cream does an average American consume every year?
4. The average American spends what percentage of his or her income on food?
5. What food do Americans like the least?

B. Listen to the newscast again for these words. Can you guess their meaning from the context?

decade
calorie conscious
sharply
disposable income
topped the list

C. *Listening Carefully:* Your teacher will read aloud the following passage. Fill in the blanks with the missing words.

According to the figures _____ (1) by the United States Department of Agriculture, the diet _____ (2) average American _____ (3) considerably in the past twenty years. Americans _____ (4) more chicken, fish, and seafood but less lamb and veal. Cheese _____ (5) favorite American food with consumption up 71 percent in the past two decades. Calorie-conscious Americans are consuming _____ (6) milk and butter _____ (7) before. _____ (8) other hand, the use of sugar _____ (9) sweeteners has climbed sharply, largely because _____ (10) 175 percent increase in soft drink consumption. The figures also show that the average American _____ (11) eighteen pounds of ice cream _____ (12) .

INTERVIEW

Use these questions as a guide to interview a classmate. Add questions of your own.

1. Has American food influenced food in your country? If so, how?
2. Has your cooking become Americanized?
3. What surprised you about American cooking?

4. What is considered a delicacy in your country? What unusual food is eaten? Do people eat pigs' intestines, eels, cockroaches, dogs, cats, rabbits, mice, tongue, frogs, snails, seaweed, or horses?

5. Describe a peasant's meal in your country. Describe a gourmet meal in your country.

6. In your country is health food popular? Is junk food popular? Are there many vegetarians?

7. Do people in your country tend to overeat?

8. Do husbands or wives generally do the cooking at home? Are the famous chefs male or female?

9. Is there a problem of malnutrition in your country?

10. Does the government have any nutritional programs (rationing, subsidies, price controls, surplus food, food stamps, free school lunches)? Explain.

7 More Men Infiltrating Professions Historically Dominated By Women

As the women's movement grows in America, men too are being freed from traditional roles. Today you see more and more men in the delivery room when their children are being born. You see American men changing diapers, taking paternity leaves, and gaining custody of their children in divorces.

Another change in men's roles has occurred in the types of professions available to them. Traditional "female" jobs such as kindergarten teacher, nurse, and secretary are now opening up to men. The following article examines this phenomenon and its effect on the professions that men have begun to "infiltrate."

MORE MEN INFILTRATING PROFESSIONS HISTORICALLY DOMINATED BY WOMEN

By CAROL HYMOWITZ

When Donald Olayer enrolled in nursing school nine years ago, his father took it hard. "Here's my father, a steelworker, hearing about other
5 steelworkers' sons who were becoming welders or getting football scholarships," Mr. Olayer recalls. "The thought of his son becoming a nurse was too much."
10 Today, Mr. Olayer, a registered nurse trained as an anesthetist, earns about $30,000 a year at Jameson Memorial Hospital in New Castle, Pa. His father, he says, has "done an
15 about-face. Now he tells the guys he works with that their sons, who can't find jobs even after four years of college, should have become nurses."

That's not an unusual turnabout
20 nowadays. Just as women have gained a footing in nearly every occupation once reserved for men, men can be found today working routinely in a wide variety of jobs once held
25 nearly exclusively by women. The men are working as receptionists and flight attendants, servants, and even "Kelly girls."

The Urban Institute, a research
30 group in Washington, recently estimated that the number of male secretaries rose 24% to 31,000 in 1978 from 25,000 in 1972, while the number of male telephone operators over the same span rose 38%, and the number 35 of male nurses, 94%. Labor experts expect the trend to continue.

Job Availability Cited

For one thing, tightness in the job market seems to have given men an 40 additional incentive to take jobs where they can find them. Although female-dominated office and service jobs for the most part rank lower in pay and status, "they're still there," 45 says June O'Neill, director of program and policy research at the institute. Traditionally male blue-collar jobs, meanwhile, "aren't increasing at all."

At the same time, she says, "the 50 outlooks of young people are different." Younger men, with less rigid views on what constitutes male or female work "may not feel there's such a stigma to working in a female- 55 dominated field."

Although views have softened, men who cross the sexual segregation line in the job market may still face discrimination and ridicule. David 60 Anderson, a 36-year-old former high school teacher, says he found secretarial work "a way out of teaching and into the business world." He had applied for work at 23 employment 65 agencies for "management training jobs that didn't exist," and he discovered that "the best skill I had was being able to type 70 words a minute."

70   He took a job as a secretary to the marketing director of a New York publishing company. But he says he could "feel a lot of people wondering what I was doing there and if something was 75 wrong with me."

Mr. Anderson's boss was a woman. When she asked him to fetch coffee, he says, "the other secretaries' eyebrows went up, and one snidely 80 said, 'Oh, there goes Kay's new boy.'" Sales executives who come in to see his boss, he says, "couldn't quite believe that I could and would type, take dictation, and answer the 85 phones."

Occasionally, men in traditionally female jobs may find themselves treated as sex objects. Anthony Shee, a flight attendant with US Air Inc., 90 says some women passengers flirt brazenly. "One lady felt compelled to pat me on the rear when I walked down the aisle," he says, "and she was traveling with her husband."

95   On the other hand, the males sometimes find themselves mistaken for higher-status professionals. Mr. Shee has been mistaken for a pilot. Mr. Anderson, the secretary, says he 100 found himself being "treated in executive tones whenever I wore a suit."

In fact, the men in traditional female jobs often move up the ladder fast. Mr. Anderson actually worked only seven months as a secretary. 105 Then he got a higher level, better-paying job as a placement counselor at an employment agency. "I got a lot of encouragement to advance," he says, "including job tips from male execu- 110 tives who couldn't quite see me staying a secretary."

Experts say, for example, that while men make up only a small fraction of elementary school teachers, a 115 disproportionate number of elementary principals are men. Barbara Bergmann, an economist at the University of Maryland who has studied sex segregation at work, believes that's 120 partly because of "sexism in the occupational structure" and partly because men have been raised to assert themselves and to assume responsibility. Men may also feel more 125 compelled than women to advance, she suspects.

Donald Olayer, the nurse, is typical. Almost as soon as he graduated from nursing school, he says he 130 decided "not to stay just a regular floor nurse earning only $12,000 a year." Now he can look forward to earning three times that much, "enough to support a family on," he 135 says, and he also has "much more responsibility."

TEST YOUR READING COMPREHENSION

A.   Based on the reading, decide whether the following statements are true or false.

1. Donald Olayer's father was proud when he first learned that his son wanted to be a nurse.
2. American society now totally accepts men in so-called "female" professions.
3. Young people are more willing to break sex segregation barriers in the job market.

4. Men were not surprised to find out that Mr. Anderson was a secretary.
5. Men are entering and advancing in "female" occupations in greater numbers.
6. Today most elementary school teachers are men.
7. Barbara Bergmann, an economist, said that men are naturally more assertive than women.
8. Donald Olayer's father was not impressed by his son's salary.

B. Which of the sentences above best states the main idea of the reading? Circle it.

C. *Vocabulary in Context:* Without using a dictionary, study how the following words or phrases are used in the reading. Work together in pairs to figure out what the words mean.

(14) an about-face
(21) gained a footing
(34) over the same span
(44) rank
(91) felt compelled
(100) in executive tones
(110) job tips

D. *Vocabulary 1:* Fill in the blanks with the correct word.

disproportionate	flirted	snidely	welders
exclusively	incentive	stigma	
fetch	infiltrated	turnabout	

1. Although she never _____ with other men, her husband was insanely jealous.

2. The government lowered interest rates as an _____ to new construction.

3. The spy _____ the enemy's headquarters and was able to warn his country of the impending attack.

4. The Friday night poker game was an _____ male gathering.

5. Experienced _____ were in great demand to work on the huge pipeline project.

6. Southern states receive a _____ share of federal contracts.

7. "You're getting married *again*?" he _____ remarked.

8. His dog was trained to _____ his slippers.

9. The senator made a complete _____ on the arms issue as election day neared.

10. The _____ of divorce is fading in America.

E. *Vocabulary 2:* Fill in the blanks with the correct word form.

1. **(secretary)** All of his _____ skills were top-notch.
2. **(sex)** The movie was banned because of its _____ explicit theme.
3. **(researcher)** He does a great deal of _____ on animals.
4. **(economy)** Even though he lost his job, he refused to _____ on food.
5. **(anesthetist)** The operation could not begin until the patient was _____ .
6. **(mistake)** On her way to a job interview, she _____ drove past the turnpike entrance.
7. **(dominate)** The president of the company had a _____ personality.
8. **(assert)** Handicapped people have become more _____ about their rights.

F. *Vocabulary 3:* Write your own sentence using the italicized phrase.

1. When Donald Olayer enrolled in nursing school nine years ago, his father *took it hard*.
2. "The thought of his son becoming a nurse was *too much*."
3. Men who cross the sexual segregation line may still *face discrimination* and ridicule.
4. *On the other hand*, the males sometimes find themselves mistaken for higher-status professionals.
5. In fact, the men in traditional female jobs often *move up the ladder* fast.

G. *Vocabulary 4:* These words are often misused. Choose the correct word and explain your choice.

1. He took a job (**as, like**) a secretary to the marketing director.
2. Female-dominated office and service jobs for (**most of the, most of, the most**) part rank lower in pay and status.
3. Sales executives "couldn't (**quit, quiet, quite**) believe that I could and would type, take dictation, and answer (**0, to**) the phone."
4. Barbara Bergmann, an economist at (**0, the, a, an**) University of Maryland, has studied sex segregation at work.
5. Men have been (**risen, raised, grown up**) to assert themselves and to assume responsibility.

RETELL THE STORY

Use the outline below as a guide to tell the story in class.

- Donald Olayer's occupation and his father's reaction
- the trend toward men doing "women's" jobs
- reasons for the trend
- the problems of men in traditionally female jobs
- examples of men moving up the ladder fast
- reasons for male advancement

SPEAK UP

1. ONE-MINUTE SPEECH: Describe a job in your native country that was once restricted to persons of one sex but is now open to both males and females. What caused the change? When did it begin to happen? Has the job gained or lost status as a result?

2. DEBATE: Should a company be permitted to refuse to hire a young married woman because it is afraid she will bcome pregnant and leave? Here are some arguments on both sides:

FOR THE COMPANY

1. The company will lose the money spent on training the woman for the job.
2. Most women who have babies don't return to work.
3. A mother's place is in the home.
4. Women with children take off too much time from work.

FOR THE WOMEN

1. Young males aren't refused employment when they marry.
2. Women today have to work to support the family.
3. Women's careers should not be penalized simply because they need to take time off for childbearing.
4. A woman today can raise a child and hold a job at the same time.

TABLE 7-1 Percentage of Women in Selected Occupations

OCCUPATION	1962	1981
Bartender	11	47
Baker	18	41
Pharmacist	10	26
Scientist	9	22
Bill collector	22	63

Refer to Table 7-1 in answering the following questions.

1. In what profession do women now outnumber men?
2. In what occupation have women shown the least improvement?

3. Do women outnumber men in any of these occupations in your country?

TEST YOUR LISTENING COMPREHENSION

A. Listen to the tape before continuing on. (The Listening Transcript appears on page 132.) Based on the listening, answer the following questions.

1. What is the percentage change in the number of working women in the past twenty years?
2. Name one job category in which women now outnumber men.
3. What percentage of lawyers are women today?
4. What percentage of engineers are women today?
5. How does the median annual salary of a full-time working woman compare with the average man's salary?
6. What is the House of Representatives planning to do this fall?

B. Listen to the newscast again for these words. Can you guess their meaning from the context?

decade
outnumber
matched
median
hearings

C. *Listening Carefully:* Your teacher will read aloud the following passage. Fill in the blanks with the missing words.

According ＿＿＿＿＿＿ study by the United States Department of
　　　　　　　　(1)

Labor, the number of working women in America ＿＿＿＿＿＿ 95 per-
　　　　　　　　　　　　　　　　　　　　　　　　　　　(2)

cent ＿＿＿＿＿＿ two decades, and many of the jobs now
　　　　(3)

＿＿＿＿＿＿ by women were once largely ＿＿＿＿＿＿ by men. In
　　(4)　　　　　　　　　　　　　　　　　　(5)

several ＿＿＿＿＿＿ categories, including insurance adjusters, real
　　　　　(6)

estate brokers, and production-line assemblers, women now outnumber

men, ＿＿＿＿＿＿ from the proportion twenty years ago. Nearly 50 per-
　　　(7)

cent of _____ bus drivers and bartenders are now women,
          (8)

_____ 10 percent twenty years ago.
     (9)

INTERVIEW

Use these questions as a guide to interview a classmate. Add questions of your own.

1. What jobs are *not* open to women in your country? (corporation executives, bankers, construction workers, architects, engineers, pilots, police officers, firefighters, soldiers, bus drivers)
2. Are there any women in high positions in government?
3. Are there laws against sex discrimination in your country? Can a woman who has suffered sex discrimination on the job take the matter to court? If not, what can she do?
4. Do married women work? Do married women with children work? Are there child-care centers for working women in your country? If there are none, what do working women do?
5. Some American companies grant paternity leaves to fathers. Does this practice exist in your country? What do you think of it? Would you (your husband) take a paternity leave?
6. Are there any jobs that you wouldn't want to see a man or woman do? Which ones and why?

8 *No Vacancy*

Have you been affected by the shortage of affordable apartments where you live? It sometimes seems as if everyone in the United States is looking for an apartment he or she can afford, from students who can't find dormitory space to senior citizens who are forced to stay with their grandchildren. As you read this article, think about whether a similar story could be written about apartment hunting in your native country.

NO VACANCY

APARTMENTS ARE SCARCE, BUT THE OUTLOOK DIMS FOR NEW CONSTRUCTION

Staying with Mom and Dad

By ANTHONY RAMIREZ

For two years, Mattie Presley has been trying to move out of her sister's house. But in Seattle, where the 24-year-old office assistant lives, almost
5 99% of the apartments are occupied, and waiting lists are long. The apartments that are left are too expensive for Miss Presley. "I'm stuck," she says.
10 In many other cities the apartment supply is almost as tight. The occupancy rate in some parts of Los Angeles is 98%. Rodney Lucio, a 23-year-old law student there, shares a
15 cramped $433-a-month apartment with two roommates. That's better than last year, when he lived out of his Toyota Celica sedan for three weeks waiting for an opening at an apart-
20 ment complex.

In Detroit, where occupancy is 97%, retired nurse Ann Jordan lives with her daughter's large family. To make room for her, two of her
25 grandchildren and a 3-year-old great-grandchild must sleep on the living room floor. "It pains me to see my family crowded so," says the 67-year-old Mrs. Jordan. But government-sub-
30 sidized apartments for the elderly have five-year waiting lists, and non-subsidized housing is far too costly.

Doubling Up

Around the country there is a growing shortage of apartments. One 35 result is that many people, usually the young and those on fixed incomes, must move in with relatives or take on roommates. The shortage is likely to worsen as the rise in interest rates 40 drives even more builders away from apartment construction.

"I'm sitting on land that's already zoned for multi-family use," says Robert Brody, a Detroit-area devel- 45 oper, whose view is typical of many builders. "I'm not going to build a thing on it until those rates come down."

Condominium conversion is grow- 50 ing, and this trend worsens the apartment shortage by reducing the supply of rental apartments and driving up rents of the remaining units.

Basically, the shortage has two 55 causes: increasing construction and operating costs and owners' declining ability to raise rents. Biltmore Homes Co., a Detroit builder, was forced to cancel a 108-unit luxury apartment 60 complex when it turned out that the firm would have to charge $705 a month in rent to recover its invest-

68

ment. "Who's going to pay that?" asks
65 Abraham Ran, vice-president of
construction.

Costs to operate a building once
it's built have also skyrocketed. A
Southern California landlord, Maxine
70 Trevethen of Rancho Palos Verdes,
complained in a letter to the *Los
Angeles Times* that her gains under
Proposition 13 were "nonexistent."
The sharp property tax cut "merely
75 allows me to cut my losses and help
pay a plumbing bill of $5,000," she
wrote. Increasingly, builders are
requiring tenants to pay for heat and
electricity. They install separate air
80 conditioning units for each apartment, even though centralized sys-
tems would be more energy efficient.

Meanwhile rents haven't kept
pace with costs. "Rents have risen
85 only about half the general rate of
inflation," says Kenneth Rosen, a
Princeton University economics professor who studies housing.

All of which is little consolation
90 for the apartment hunter. "I get mad
every day," says Kathy Rowe, who's
been looking a month for an apartment in Atlanta, where the occupancy
rate is about 98%. "If the newspaper
95 ads say call after 6 P.M. and you call at
6:13, you miss the apartment." Miss
Rowe, a 28-year-old psychology
research assistant, tries to outfox
rival apartment seekers by buying the
100 first edition of the Sunday newspaper
on Saturday night for an early peek at
the ads. "But that's what everyone
else is probably doing," she concedes.

"I'm just biding my time," says
105 Miss Presley in Seattle. At one complex she's next in line for a $185-dol-
lar-a-month, two-bedroom apartment.

She's waiting for a couple to move out
when their new home is completed.

Worrying About the Rent   110

But she worries about paying the
rent, which would be nearly 43% of
her $435 a month take-home salary.
She's unmarried and has a five-year-
old son. "I'm just going to have to let a   115
lot of things go," she says, like eating
out, a weekly bowling night, and an
occasional movie ticket.

In Hackensack, N.J., 22-year-old
Rosemary Inbemba is living with her   120
parents to save money. Rent for an
apartment by herself, she figures,
would eat up half of her $8,000 take-
home salary as a housing counselor. If
she moved out of her parents' house,   125
she says, "I'd have to take a part-time
job, forget graduate school, forget new
clothes, forget purchasing a car, and
forget socializing."

For some young people having to   130
live at home has yielded unexpected
rewards. "I appreciate my parents a
lot more," says Jeanne Mori, a 23-
year-old fine arts graduate student at
UCLA. "I'm not into the big independ-   135
ence struggle anymore, and living at
home has made me realize that my
parents are really okay."

For the elderly, though, it's often
frustrating to live with their children.   140
"I've always been independent," says
Mrs. Jordan in Detroit. "My family
doesn't want me to live alone, but I
prefer to be alone." Mrs. Jordan has
traveled all over town looking for low-   145
rent housing, where older citizens pay
$100 or less in rent. At one such apart-
ment complex, she was told the waiting list had 800 names.

TEST YOUR READING COMPREHENSION

A. Based on the reading, decide whether the following statements are true or false.

1. There is a shortage of affordable apartments in many American cities.
2. According to the article, the supply of apartments will increase when interest rates go up.
3. Waiting lists are long for government-subsidized housing.
4. Builders are not building new apartments because of a shortage of land.
5. There has been a growth in the construction of new apartments.
6. Condominium conversion has little effect on the apartment shortage.
7. Some young people, such as Jeanne Mori, like living at home.
8. The elderly don't always want to live with their children.

B. Which of the sentences above best states the main idea of the reading? Circle it.

C. *Vocabulary in Context:* Without using a dictionary, study how the following words and phrases are used in the reading. Work together in pairs to figure out what the words mean.

(18) sedan
(20) complex
(43) I'm sitting on land
(73) Proposition 13
(104) I'm just biding my time

D. *Vocabulary 1:* Fill in the blanks with the correct word.

cramped	skyrocketed	subsidized	took on
peeked	stuck	tight	yielded

1. After working on the math problem for one hour, he told his teacher he was _____ .

2. There is an oversupply of engineers which has made the job market very _____ .

3. The tall man felt _____ in the airplane seat.

4. To help the wheat farmers, the government has _____ the price of fertilizer.

5. She _____ so many jobs that she had little time for herself.

6. Because of inflation, the cost of buying a house has _____ .

7. Advances in medicine and nutrition have _____ a longer life for the average American.

8. The frightened boy _____ through the window before opening the door.

E. *Vocabulary 2:* Fill in the blanks with the correct word form.

1. (worse)   This is the _____ he's ever done on a test.

2. (plumbing)   When the toilet broke, they called a _____ .

3. (install)   The store promised free _____ with the purchase of a new air conditioner.

4. (reward)   What a _____ experience to have been a student in his class!

5. (cost)   New cars have become quite _____ recently.

6. (social)   She enjoyed _____ with her students after class.

7. (rival)   The _____ between the two teams goes back for years.

8. (drive)   _____ away by his harsh words, she swore she would never see him again.

9. (marry)   Her mother told her not to go out with a _____ man.

10. (subsidize)   The senator supported a federal _____ for the steel industry.

F. *Vocabulary 3:* Write your own sentence using the italicized phrase.

1. Miss Rowe, a 28-year-old psychology research assistant, *tries to outfox* rival apartment seekers by buying the first edition of the Sunday newspaper on Saturday night for an early peek at the ads.
2. "*I'm not into* the big independence struggle anymore, and living at home has made me realize that my parents are really okay."
3. The apartments that are left are too expensive for Miss Presley. "*I'm stuck,*" she says.
4. The rise in interest rates *drives* even more builders *away.*

G. *Vocabulary 4:* These words are often misused. Choose the correct word and explain your choice.

1. That's better (**then, than**) last year.
2. Government subsidized apartments have (**five year, five years, five-year, five-years**) waiting lists.
3. (**Whose, Who's**) going to pay that?
4. Costs to operate a building once (**its, it's**) built have also skyrocketed.

5. Kenneth Rosen is a Princeton University (**economy, economic, economics, economical**) professor.

6. If she moved out of her (**parent's , parents, parents'**) house, she says, "I'd have to take a part-time job."

RETELL THE STORY

Use the outline below as a guide to tell the story in class.

THE PROBLEM OF FINDING AN AFFORDABLE APARTMENT

- law student who had to live in a Toyota
- grandmother living with her daughter's family

THE CAUSE OF THE SHORTAGE

- rising building costs
- rising operating costs
- condominium conversions

HOW SOME PEOPLE ARE COPING

- how to outfox other apartment hunters
- benefits of living at home

SPEAK UP

1. ONE-MINUTE SPEECH: Give a detailed description of your house or apartment. Describe the layout, the neighborhood, interesting features and drawbacks.

2. ROLE PLAY: *Apartment Seeker and Real Estate Broker.* You are looking for an apartment. Ask the real estate agent about the following: location, cost, room size, broker's fee, furnished, unfurnished, doorman, safety, intercom system, elevator, transportation, sunlight, ceilings, heat and electricity, air conditioning, appliances, laundry, neighborhood, renovation, security deposit, and lease. Use the expressions below.

I'm interested in the three-bedroom apartment on the East Side in the 80's.

Is the apartment still available?

When can I see it?

What is the neighborhood like?

How long is the lease for?

How much is the rent?

Are utilities included?

3. ROLE PLAY: *Tenant and Landlord.* It's 30 degrees outside and snowing. You haven't had any heat or hot water in two days. Complain to your landlord. Describe other serious problems in your apartment as well. Use the expressions below.

FOR THE TENANT:

What's taking so long?
Why hasn't it been fixed yet?
You've got to . . .

FOR THE LANDLORD:

We'll see what we can do.
I'll get on it right away.
I'll take care of it as soon as I can.
I'm trying my best.
You've got to wait.
The boiler's broken.

TABLE 8-1   Selected Housing Characteristics From the 1980 Census

Total housing units	88,411,263
Owner-occupied housing units	51,794,545
Total year-round housing units	86,769,389
No bathroom or only half a bath	2,880,165
1 complete bathroom plus half bath(s)	50,534,847
2 or more complete bathrooms	21,019,978
No air conditioning	39,179,172
Central system of air conditioning	23,628,263
1 or more individual room units air conditioned	23,961,954
With telephone	74,713,495
Without telephone	5,676,178

Refer to Table 8-1 in answering the following questions.

1. Do most American families live in rented apartments?
2. How many American homes have two or more bathrooms?
3. Do most American homes have some form of air conditioning?

TEST YOUR LISTENING COMPREHENSION

A. Listen to the tape before continuing on. (The Listening Transcript appears on page 133.) Based on the listening, answer the following questions.

1. What is the temperature in the New York metropolitan area?
2. How many heat complaints were received yesterday?

ALTERNATIVE SPACES

Pothole Estates

Junior Studio

Two-Bedroom Kayak

Basement Single

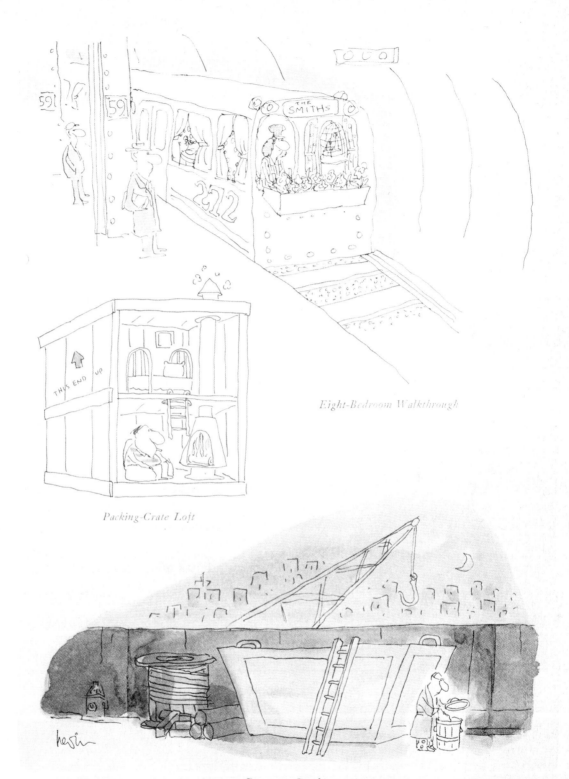

Eight-Bedroom Walkthrough

Packing-Crate Loft

Dumpster Duplex

3. How much can a landlord be fined for not providing heat?
4. If you have a heat complaint, what number do you call?
5. What did the landlord plead guilty to?
6. What was the judge's sentence?
7. Did the landlord go to court willingly?

B. Listen to the newscast again for these words. Can you guess their meaning from the context?

deliberately
withholding
cots
handcuffs
summonses

C. *Listening Carefully:* Your teacher will read aloud the following passage. Fill in the blanks with the missing words.

And in a related story, a landlord who pleaded guilty to deliberately

withholding heat from his tenants was _____ spend four nights
(1)

_____ emergency tenant shelter _____ go to jail.
(2) (3)

Judge Randolph Carr _____ landlord, John Lawson,
(4)

_____ stay in the shelter _____ with cots and blankets
(5) (6)

for families with heatless apartments, _____ him an opportunity
(7)

to meet many of the residents in his community _____ to obtain
(8)

emergency housing because landlords did not provide sufficient heat. Mr.

Lawson, _____ $2,000 by Judge Carr, was brought into court in
(9)

handcuffs when he _____ answer several summonses
(10)

_____ his building.
(11)

INTERVIEW _____

Use these questions as a guide to interview a classmate. Add questions of your own.

1. How hard is it to find an apartment in your country? How do you go about it?

2. Do any of the following people have a special problem in your country in finding an apartment: an unmarried woman, an unmarried man, a divorced woman, a single parent, a couple with children, an elderly couple, a foreigner, a tenant with a pet, a person from a religious minority, a homosexual, a student, a smoker?

3. Describe a typical apartment. How does it differ from an apartment in the United States (size, appliances, cost, comfort)? What part of your take-home salary goes toward the rent?

4. Does your government subsidize housing for the poor, the elderly, the handicapped, the unemployed, or the lower-middle-class? Explain.

5. Are rents controlled by the government? What do you think of this policy?

6. Describe your personal experience in finding a place to live here.

7. Describe any problems you have had as a tenant or as a landlord. How was the problem resolved?

9 *Literacy in America*

MANY OF YOUR NEIGHBORS CAN'T

READ THIS

Over half a million adult New Yorkers cannot read prescription labels, street maps, or job applications.

Reading help is available to them through Literacy Volunteers of New York City. The organization recruits, trains and supervises volunteer tutors, who in turn provide free, one-to-one tutoring to adult students.

 Literacy Volunteers asks that a volunteer tutor take an 18-hour training workshop and then tutor one adult two hours per week, for a minimum of 50 hours. No teaching experience is required.

The next training workshop will be offered in Brooklyn Heights at the First Presbyterian Church, 124 Henry Street, April 27 and 29, and May 6, 11, 13, and 18 from 6 to 9 p.m.

Please call the number below for further information.

HELP
SOMEONE LEARN TO READ
in
Brooklyn Heights
CALL: LITERACY VOLUNTEERS OF NYC
522-0320

Used by permission of the *Literacy Volunteers of New York City*.

While hundreds of thousands of foreigners from all over the world come to the United States to study at America's renowned universities, the American educational system has been unable to solve the problem of functional illiteracy. The following article explores the historical causes of this phenomenon.

LITERACY IN AMERICA

By ANTHONY BRANDT

OSSINING, N.Y.—We hear a great deal about the literacy crisis, and a great deal of criticism has been directed at the educational system for causing it.

Some 23 million adult Americans are "functionally illiterate," unable to read newspapers or fill out job application forms, and the schools regularly produce large numbers of students who cannot pass easy minimum-competency tests. Critics lay the blame variously upon poor teaching, on ill-advised teaching methods such as the "look-and-say" method for teaching children to read, and on the long trend in education away from the basics, a trend that reached its peak in the 1960's and early 1970's.

The problem, however, may have less to do with the educational system than with the changes in public values.

Almost from the beginning of the settlement of this country, Americans were known for enjoying unusually high levels of literacy.

By 1765 John Adams could claim that "A native of America who cannot read or write is as rare an appearance as . . . a comet or an earthquake."

Adams' statement reflected the especially high literacy in his own New England, where Puritan ideology predominated; the Puritans believed strongly in the value of access to the Bible, to the Work of God, and to that end went to great lengths to make sure that their children were literate. Servant indentures required masters to teach their servants and apprentices to read and write if they could not already do so. Families were examined regularly by Puritan divines to see whether parents were teaching their children to read and write. The New England Colonies established schools everywhere that the population was concentrated enough to support them. Historians attribute this zeal for literacy almost entirely to Puritanism; a Puritan had to be able to read to gain direct access to the Word and save his unregenerate soul from the vividly imagined fires of Hell.

Later, when religious feeling declined, literacy became a way up and out of one's economic or social circumstances. If one wanted to rise, to become involved in the nation's political life, to master the complexities of an increasingly industrialized environment, it was essential to be literate. The educational system of the late 18th and 19th centuries was much poorer than what we have today, all talk about little red schoolhouses notwithstanding: the quality of teaching was low, facilities were grossly inadequate, and many children did not attend school at all. Yet by 1850 the adult literacy rate for both males and females had reached 90 percent. That was higher than the rate in any European country except Sweden; it was also considerably higher than the percentage of children attending school. The country was full of self-made readers and writers, people who had struggled to become literate but for whom the struggle had real meaning and definite rewards.

Continued on Page 80, Column 1

The meaning is still there, and rewards are still available, but we no longer seem to care. For whatever reason—television, widespread anomie, the anti-intellectualism that is also part of our history—we don't value literacy as we once did. The public worries about the high rates of functional illiteracy and talks nostalgically about a return to the three R's,* but that same public spends an average of nearly 30 hours a week per person watching television. Half of that public, according to a survey by the Book Industry Study Group, never reads any kind of book; and it writes prose, when it writes at all, that has led to talk of a "writing crisis" on top of the literacy crisis.

This loss of commitment to literacy comes at a time when the demand for higher and higher levels of literacy is growing. Yesterday's functional literacy is dysfunctional today. Jobs require more education today, not less; high technology and an increasingly bureaucratized way of life demand more reading, more writing than ever. In 1939 the Navy's most sophisticated weapons system came with a technical manual of 500 pages. Its most advanced system in 1978 came with 300,000 pages of documentation. In spite of what Marshall McLuhan and other prophets of a printless society may claim, literacy remains indispensable.

What the history of literacy demonstrates is that preserving literacy is not and never has been a function that belongs solely to the schools. A highly literate society evolves out of deeply held values, values that cannot be isolated in a school system but must permeate the whole society.

Unless we recover those values, we put ourselves in serious danger. "If a nation expects to be ignorant and free, in a state of civilization," wrote Thomas Jefferson, "it expects what never was and what never will be."

*reading, writing, and arithmetic (Editor's note)

TEST YOUR READING COMPREHENSION

A. Based on the reading, decide whether the following statements are true or false.

1. The literacy problem in the United States is solely the result of poor teaching methods.
2. Today's functional illiteracy is a result of a change in public values.
3. Twenty-three million adults are completely illiterate in the United States.
4. Anyone who goes to school is not functionally illiterate.
5. Puritanism encouraged literacy in the late 18th century.
6. The educational system was better in the 18th and 19th centuries than it is today.
7. There were many self-made readers and writers in the late 19th century.
8. Half of the people in the United States don't read books.
9. Literacy is not as necessary as it once was.

10. According to Thomas Jefferson, it is impossible to be ignorant and free.

B.   Which of the sentences above best states the main idea of the reading? Circle it.

C.   *Vocabulary in Context:* Without using a dictionary, study how the following words or phrases are used in the reading. Work together in pairs to figure out what the words mean.

(7) functionally illiterate
(30) as rare an appearance as a comet or an earthquake
(34) Puritan ideology
(68) notwithstanding

D.   *Vocabulary 1:* Fill in the blanks with the correct word.

apprentice	indispensable	permeated	zeal
commitment	nostalgic	self-made	
grossly	peak	widespread	

1. Elvis Presley reached his _____ of popularity in the late fifties.

2. Instead of going to cooking school, he decided to become an _____ to a chef.

3. Teaching those students was exciting because of their _____ for learning.

4. He felt that whenever she told a story, she _____ exaggerated the details.

5. Having never gone to school, he considered himself a _____ man.

6. The odor of fresh paint _____ the new apartment.

7. He felt _____ about the town where he was born.

8. The candidate's strong _____ to help the elderly will improve his chances of winning the election.

9. The mayor's popularity was _____ until he raised taxes.

10. A strong rope is _____ for safe rock climbing.

E.   *Vocabulary 2:* Fill in the blanks with the correct word form.

1. **(politics)**   Although she didn't consider herself

    _____ , she went to the demonstration against nuclear power.

2. **(economy)**   They bought a second-hand car because it was
                          more _____ .

3. **(loss)**   Don't _____ your keys!

4. **(deep)**   He spoke to me about the problems in his country
                          in great _____ .

5. **(lead)**   Who _____ the country into World War
                          II?

6. **(literate)**   The government is sponsoring a _____
                          campaign.

7. **(critic)**   He was overly _____ of his oldest son.

8. **(competency)**   After two years of training as a carpenter, he felt
                          _____ to take on the job.

F. *Vocabulary 3:* Write your own sentence using the italicized phrase.

1. The Puritans believed strongly in the value of access to the Bible and
    to that end *went to great lengths* to make sure that their children were
    literate.
2. Later, when religious feeling declined, literacy became *a way up* and
    out of one's economic or social circumstances.
3. If one wanted to rise, *it was essential to* be literate.
4. The public *worries about* the high rates of functional illiteracy.

G. *Vocabulary 4:* These words are often misused. Choose the correct word and explain
your choice.

1. Some 23 (**millions, million**) adult Americans are "functionally
    illiterate."
2. Schools regularly produce large (**numbers, amounts**) of students who
    cannot pass easy minimum-competency tests.
3. The country was full of self-made readers and writers, people for (**who,
    whom**) the struggle to become literate had real meaning.
4. This (**lose, loss, lost, loose**) of commitment to literacy comes when the
    demand for higher levels of literacy is growing.

RETELL THE STORY

Use the outline below as a guide to tell the story in class.

- the literacy problem today
- the Puritan influence

- what happened when religious feelings declined
- the change in public values
- the need for literacy
- the result of illiteracy

SPEAK UP

1. **ONE-MINUTE SPEECH:** Give a resume of your education including a short description of the schools you attended. Also mention any present educational plans you have. Use the expressions below as necessary.

   graduated from
   receive a B.A. (an M.A., an M.B.A., a Ph.D)
   have a degree in _____
   majored in
   coed
   working on
   study at a university
   a two-year program in
   a certificate in
   I'm a licensed _____
   I apprenticed in _____

2. **ROLE PLAY:** *Career Counselor and Student.* Do you need advice on your career goals and educational plans? See a career counselor. Describe in detail what your career goals are and ask for advice. Use the expressions below.

STUDENT	COUNSELOR
I'm planning to....	I suggest (recommend) your going....
I intend to....	
My plan is to....	I suggest (recommend) that you go....
I'm thinking of....	
What I have in mind is....	I advise you to go....

3. **RESEARCH AND TELL:** Report what you know about these men: Thomas Jefferson, John Adams, and Marshall McLuhan. Go to the library and find out why they are famous.

TABLE 9-1 Rates of University Attendance for Selected Countries

COUNTRY	PERCENTAGE OF POPULATION IN COLLEGE (IN A SINGLE YEAR)
United States	5.2
Canada	3.6
Argentina	2.4
Israel	2.3
Japan	2.2
France	2.1
Venezuela	2.0
Soviet Union	2.0
Italy	1.9
Poland	1.8
West Germany	1.7
Egypt	1.4
Britain	1.3
Brazil	1.3
Mexico	1.0
South Korea	1.0

Refer to Table 9-1 in answering the following questions.

1. Which European country has the highest percentage of its population in college?
2. If your native country is not on this list, where do you think it would rate?

TEST YOUR LISTENING COMPREHENSION

A. Listen to the tape before continuing on. (The Listening Transcript begins on page 133.) Based on the listening, answer the following questions.

1. Who prepared the study on college education?
2. Do a higher proportion of people go to college in the Soviet Union than in the United States?
3. How many college students are there today in the United States?
4. What percentage of the student population is female?
5. What percentage of the student population is black?
6. Why is part-time enrollment growing?
7. What percentage of the student population is foreign?
8. How much money do foreign students bring into the American economy?

B. Listen to the newscast again for these words. Can you guess their meaning from the context?

attained

a record high

steep rises

turn more students away

recruit

potential

influx

C. *Listening Carefully:* Your teacher will read aloud the following passages. Fill in the blanks with the missing words.

According _____ (1) United Nations study released today, a college education is _____ (2) attained _____ (3) United States _____ (4) nation. The U.N. report showed that fifty-two _____ (5) one thousand Americans attended a college or university this year. The proportion of _____ (6) enrolled in colleges and universities was 300 percent _____ (7) Great Britian and 160 percent _____ (8) Soviet Union. The report said that 12.3 _____ (9) students, _____ (10) record high of 300,000 _____ (11) students, attended American colleges this year.

INTERVIEW

Use these questions as a guide to interview a classmate. Add questions of your own.

1. Is there compulsory education in your country? Until what age? How much is tuition? Is public school open to all children in your country (even aliens)?
2. Is illiteracy a problem? Does the government have a program to combat illiteracy?
3. Is there any program for adults to get a higher education while working (continuing education)? If so, describe what subjects are available.
4. When must a student choose a career?
5. At what age do nationwide exams begin? What are they like?

6. Are there "Ivy League" schools in your country? What are the entrance requirements?

7. How much does a college education cost?

8. Are there any special programs for handicapped students or for very bright children?

9. From what you know about education in the United States, how does education differ in your country? (teacher/student relationship, dress, discipline, homework, punctuality, class participation, opportunities for men and women)

10. How would you like to see the education system in your country changed?

10 When in Japan, Do as the Japanese Do, By Speaking English

THE AMERICAN
LANGUAGE INSTITUTE

1

English is the native language of over 325 million people. It has also become the language of diplomacy and business. Its influences are apparent in medical and computer jargon, as well as in advertising and popular music. Here is the story of one group of people eager to soak up as much English as possible.

WHEN IN JAPAN, DO AS THE JAPANESE DO, BY SPEAKING ENGLISH

LANGUAGE IS STUDIED BY MANY WHO PRACTICE ON 'NATIVES'; HOW TO OBTAIN FREE COFFEE

By URBAN C. LEHNER

TOKYO—A radio network here, Nihon Shortwave Broadcasting Co., tried an experiment recently. To enliven its presentation of a Saturday-afternoon baseball game between the Yomiuri Giants and the Hansin Tigers, it broadcast every other inning in English.

An American broadcaster beaming baseball in Japanese would quickly lose his audience, but no such fate befell NSB. Of the 50 listeners who called in, 35 said they welcomed the chance to listen to the game and practice their English at the same time.

As that incident implies, Japan is once again on a learn-English binge. In contrast to the U.S., where the study of Japanese is about as popular as the study of rare fungus cultures, here fully 11% of the adults responding to one recent poll said they attend English-conversation classes. (Almost all these adults have already had at least six years of English in public school.)

"In the last several years, interest in the English language has been constantly increasing," says Naomitsu Kurnabe, a college professor and official of Japan's Institute for Research in Language Teaching.

Signs Are Everywhere

The signs of this interest are everywhere. Here in Tokyo, the number of Berlitz-type schools teaching foreign languages, mainly English, climbed by 164% between 1969 and 1979, to 396 from 150. Some large companies, such as Matsushita Electric Industrial Co. and Suntory Ltd., the whisky, beer and soft-drink maker, have recruited foreigners to teach English to their employees. There are English lessons on television and English-instruction periodicals on newsstands.

The periodicals include a tabloid newspaper called *Student Times* that carries news in both English and Japanese and has special columns explaining the meaning of such English expressions as "moonlighting" and "on the fritz."

A "native English speaker" from Britain or the U.S. who finds himself penniless in Tokyo need never suffer caffeine deprivation. "English speaking" tearooms have begun sprouting up here in the last two or three years. The idea is to give students of English a chance to practice their conversational skills in a social setting. "Native English speakers" get their coffee or tea gratis or for a nominal sum just as girls used to be admitted to some dance halls free.

More ambitious native English-speaking expatriates can keep themselves in rice and sake by teaching English—and thousands do. Many of the private schools hire almost any native English speaker, regardless of teaching ability.

A Tourist Is Waylaid

Even American tourists occasionally experience the Japanese interest in English firsthand. One American woman recently was accosted in her hotel lobby by three young Japanese men identifying themselves as medical students who insisted on buying her a drink. Their intentions turned out to be honorable, albeit somewhat unusual: they just wanted to tape-record her cocktail conversation so that they would have a native English speaker to mimic in practicing their English.

This isn't the first time the Japanese have gone on an English kick. The language has been required in public schools since Japan was "opened" in the 1860's. Interest swelled after World War II when American troops occupied Japan, and in 1964, when the Tokyo Olympic Games attracted flocks of foreign tourists.

The current English resurgence reflects a growing tendency among the Japanese to look beyond their own insular borders. Polls suggest that interest in foreign travel, both for business and for pleasure, is the most important motive this time.

"More than ever before, the Japanese have become international-minded, consumed with a desire to communicate with the outside world," says the Rev. Peter Milward, a Jesuit priest who has been teaching English in Japan for 26 years. "And for them, communication with the outside world means knowledge of today's international language, English."

According to the Japan Travel Bureau, 4 million Japanese traveled overseas in 1979, up from 3.5 million in 1978 and only 663,000 in 1970. About 20% of the travelers are on business, the government agency says.

But many students of English have no immediate plans to use it in business or tourism. Some are studying it because they are studious by nature and English is as good a subject as any. Others study it out of a vague sense of obligation to become more "international-minded" or because they consider English "prestigious" (brand names of many products, including autos, are still written in English rather than Japanese for that reason) or out of some other equally indirect motive. "English," says a research chemist for Sumitomo Chemical Co., "is my hobby."

It isn't an easy hobby for the Japanese, quite apart from their notorious difficulties in pronouncing the English "r" and "l," neither of which sounds occurs in Japanese. Namiji Itabashi, who runs one of the oldest and largest English-teaching schools, the 2,000 student Japan-American Conversation Institute, notes that many English vowel sounds don't occur in Japanese, either, and are difficult for Japanese speakers to say.

One sign that the current resurgence of English may be serious is the growing public pressure to improve public-school English education. Despite the minimum of six years the Japanese spend in junior high school and high school studying English, only 8% of Japanese adults say they can carry on a conversation with an English-speaking foreigner.

Continued on Page 90, Column 1

160 The public-school English instruction aims mainly to prepare students for college entrance examinations that focus on ability to read English and on the fine points of English grammar. Little emphasis is put on conver-165 sation. As a result, says Mr. Itabashi, the average Japanese "knows that a third-person singular subject takes an 's' at the end of the verb—but he'll still say, 'John go to the store.' "

The ministry of education, re-170 sponding to such criticism, plans to change matters over the next several years. "We have been too grammar-conscious," says Teruo Sasaki, the ministry's English specialist. The new 175 approach, he says, will emphasize "speaking, hearing, reading, and writing." Some teachers are being retrained now, he says, to improve their conversational skills. 180

TEST YOUR READING COMPREHENSION

A. Based on the reading, decide whether the following statements are true or false.

1. Japanese only study English because they have to.
2. Americans never get an opportunity to speak English in Japan.
3. Many Japanese are avidly interested in learning English because they have become more internationally minded.
4. All television programs in Japan are broadcast in Japanese and English.
5. It would be impossible for an inexperienced teacher to teach English in a private school in Japan.
6. Americans are very interested in learning Japanese.
7. Some Japanese study English because they feel it's prestigious.
8. In some English-speaking tearooms native speakers of English can get coffee or tea for free.
9. Japanese schoolchildren have good conversational skills in English.

B. Which of the sentences above best states the main idea of the reading? Circle it.

C. *Vocabulary in Context:* Without using a dictionary, study how the following words or phrases are used in the reading. Work together in pairs to figure out what the words mean.

(11) no such fate befell
(19) as popular as the study of rare fungus cultures
(58) sprouting up
(68) keep themselves in rice and sake
(74) waylaid
(96) flocks of

D. *Vocabulary 1:* Fill in the blank with the correct word.

accosted	mimic	penniless	vague
carry on	moonlighting	poll	
expatriate	motive	recruit	

1. Although the preelection _____ showed him to be losing, the candidate won by a landslide.

2. The parrot was a good _____ of his trainer's voice.

3. Hemingway was part of a large group of _____ American writers living in Paris in the twenties.

4. Large corporations visit universities to _____ employees for their companies.

5. She spoke so little English that it was difficult to _____ a conversation with her.

6. His directions were so _____ that we got lost three times on the way to his house.

7. To keep up with inflation, more and more policemen are _____ these days as security guards.

8. He woke up _____ in a strange city and had to hitchhike home.

9. He was _____ by a beggar on the street.

10. The detective suspected that the murderer's _____ was revenge.

E. *Vocabulary 2:* Fill in the blanks with the correct word form.

1. **(study)** The quiet, _____ boy was liked by all his teachers.

2. **(prestige)** Competition is intense for admission to _____ universities.

3. **(notoriety)** The actor was _____ for missing rehearsals.

4. **(critic)** Crowds flocked to the _____ acclaimed play.

5. **(intention)** The judge ruled that the murder was _____ .

6. **(vague)** I haven't the _____ idea what she meant by that remark.

7. **(occur)** An eclipse of the moon is a rare _____ .

8. **(imply)**   She considered his silence an _____ criticism of her idea.

9. **(swell)**   He took one look at her _____ ankle and rushed her to the hospital.

F.   *Vocabulary 3:* Write your own sentence using the italicized phrase.

1. Japan is once again *on a* learn English *binge.*
2. This isn't the first time the Japanese have gone *on an* English *kick.*
3. Three young Japanese men, identifying themselves as medical students, *insisted on* buy*ing* her a drink.
4. Many of the private schools will hire almost any native English speaker, *regardless of* teaching ability.
5. Even American tourists occasionally *experience* the Japanese interest in English *firsthand.*
6. Their intentions *turned out* to be honorable.

G.   *Vocabulary 4:* **These words are often misused. Choose the correct word and explain your choice.**

1. There are English lessons (**in, on**) television.
2. Interest swelled after (**a, the, Ø**) World War II.
3. They identified themselves (**like, as**) medical students.
4. An American broadcaster beaming baseball in Japanese would quickly (**loose, lose, lost**) his audience.
5. (**The most, Most, Almost**) all these adults have already had at least six years of English in public school.
6. One sign that the current resurgence of English (**maybe, may be**) serious is the growing public pressure to improve public-school English education.
7. "We have been (**to, too, too much**) grammar-conscious."

RETELL THE STORY

Use the outline below as a guide to retell the story in class.

- the baseball game on television
- signs of the English language binge: schools, companies, a newspaper, tearooms, English teachers, American tourists
- interest in English in the past
- why the Japanese study English
- problems in learning English
- problems in public schools
- plans to improve English instruction

SPEAK UP

1. ONE-MINUTE SPEECH: How long have you studied English? How much longer do you intend to study English? What helped you the most in your study of English? What advice would you give to someone just beginning to study English? Use the expressions below.

    I would suggest that he go . . . .
    I would suggest his going . . . .
    I would recommend that she study . . . .
    I would recommend her studying . . . .
    I would advise that she take . . . .
    I would advise him to take . . . .

2. ROLE PLAY: Teacher and Student.* Teach another member of your class to say some phrases in your language such as: yes, no, hello, good-bye, how are you, please, thank you, and I love you. Use the expressions below.

    It sounds like . . . .
    Repeat after me.
    Put the accent (stress) on . . . .
    It's more (less) nasal.
    You haven't quite got it.
    Roll your "r."
    That's better.
    I think you need more work on . . . .
    That's great (fantastic, wonderful, terrific).
    You sound like a native.

TABLE 10-1   How Fast Are Languages Spoken?

LANGUAGE	AVERAGE RATE OF SPEED (SYLLABLES PER MINUTE)
French	350
Japanese	310
German	250
English	220
Most languages of the South Seas	50

Refer to Table 10-1 in answering the following questions.

1. How does the speed of your native language compare with that of English?
2. Do people in your country speak at different speeds depending upon where they grew up?

*If students in the class all speak the same native language, teach the instructor.

TEST YOUR LISTENING
COMPREHENSION

A. **Listen to the tape before continuing on. (The Listening Transcript appears on page 134.) Based on the listening, answer the following questions.**

1. What did the report criticize?
2. Do many American businessmen in Japan speak Japanese well?
3. How does the problem affect the U.S. trade balance?
4. What percentage of high school students in the United States study a foreign language?
5. Do most American colleges require a foreign language for admission?
6. Why has the French government banned some English words?
7. Name two of the banned words.

B. **Listen to the newscast again for these words. Can you guess the meaning from the context?**

scandalous incompetence
a working knowledge of
a deficit
banned

C. *Listening Carefully:* **Your teacher will read the following passage. Fill in the blanks with the missing words.**

And in Paris _____ government _____ banned the use
             (1)   (2)

of 127 English words _____ protect _____ language
                          (3)   (4)

_____ foreign intruders. Public establishments _____
     (5)   (6)

50 francs (about 7 dollars) every time the use one of the _____.
                                              (7)

Words _____ include "pay TV," "jet," "jogging," and "hot dog."
        (8)

INTERVIEW

Use these questions as a guide to interview a classmate. Add questions of your own.

1. Which words from your native language have become part of American English?
2. What English words are used in your language? (in commercials, in fashion, in sports, in music, in technology, in food)

3. In Mexico the government is trying to ban the use of the apostrophe. It is not supposed to be used in Spanish, but many stores and restaurants add an apostrophe to Spanish names because they believe it sounds fashionable. Is there a similar dispute in your country over the Americanization of your language? How do you feel about it?

4. Did you "Americanize" your name when you came to the United States? Why or why not?

5. Compare the English language with your native language. What are the similarities and differences: alphabet, sounds, grammar, complexity, directness, and politeness.

11 Hazy Issue in Alaska: How Big a Pot Crop Gardeners Can Grow

Americans call their country the "land of the free." The right to think or act independently in the privacy of one's home is a cherished ideal. Yet Americans have also prided themselves on their respect for law and order. This article examines what happened in Alaska when these two American ideas clashed over the right to grow backyard marijuana.

HAZY ISSUE IN ALASKA: HOW BIG A POT CROP GARDENERS CAN GROW

By KENNETH G. SLOCUM

ANCHORAGE—The grand jury didn't have to waste much time arguing over the raw facts in the case. The man had grown 350 large marijuana plants in
5 his greenhouse, and he didn't dispute it.

The only question was whether the 50-pound harvest was for the grower's personal use, which is legal
10 in Alaska, or whether it was for sale, which isn't.

"Fifty pounds is an enourmous amount of marijuana," says Larry Weeks, Anchorage's district attorney,
15 leaving no doubt that he believed the bulkiness of the evidence, by itself, maintained a clear intent "to distribute."

The grand jury thought otherwise
20 and refused to indict the indoor gardener.

That's the way things are going these days up here in caribou country. Despite its back-country sourdough
25 image, this state is definitely the new frontier when it comes to marijuana laws.

Alaska is the only state in the nation where a person can't be prose-
30 cuted for growing and possessing marijuana at home for personal use. It's been that way since 1975, when the Alaska supreme court in Ravin vs. Alaska decided that police enforce-
35 ment in homes of a law prohibiting marijuana possession violated Alaskans' constitutional right to privacy. In effect, the decision legalized home cultivation, smoking, and possession of marijuana.
40

A Problem for Lawmen

But the court didn't say how much was too much, and therein lies a problem that is being wrestled with by both lawmen and legislators these
45 days. Without specific evidence of a marijuana possessor's intent to sell it, law enforcement people are finding it nearly impossible to successfully prosecute solely on the basis of
50 seizures of large quantities of pot.

Take the case of Neil N. Van Camp, a longshoreman who was indicted here last fall. His backyard "hothouses" were verdant with sin-
55 semilla, a potent and much-prized variety of marijuana, enough to make more than 20,000 cigarettes, according to one lawman.

The prosecutor told the jury that
60 Mr. Van Camp's family of four couldn't possibly smoke that much, so, he said, the amount circumstantially indicated an intent to sell.

The defendant and his family
65 argued otherwise. "I use it a lot in cooking," declared one of the Van Camps. "It's great in granola, cookies, and spice cake."

Moreover, contended Mr. Van
70 Camp's attorney, his client was a man of excesses. He "smokes like a chim-

Continued on Page 98, Column 1

ney," the lawyer said, and used to drink "like a damned fish."

75   The jury acquitted Mr. Van Camp.

Despite such tolerant views by juries, Alaska is far from hazy with marijuana smoke. There's still a civil penalty of up to a $100 fine to possess
80   an ounce of pot in public; it's a misdemeanor to use it in public and a felony to sell it.

Lessened Guilt Feelings

Moreover, says Mike Rubenstein,
85   executive director of the Alaska Judicial Council, "I don't believe anybody living in Alaska has formed the opinion that there was any change whatsoever in the incidence of marijuana use
90   as a result of the supreme court decision. The most that happened was that it probably made people feel better in that they were no longer breaking the law in smoking marijuana at
95   home." The Alaska Judicial Council is a state body that studies the administration of justice and makes recommendations to the Supreme Court and the state legislature.

100   Nor is the added freedom to puff pot having a discernible effect on schools, local people say. "School counselors tell me there was greater use of marijuana in the schools in the
105   1960's than there is now," says John B. Peper, superintendent of schools for the Anchorage area. "The present generation is less interested in being rebellious—there was a hard-rock,
110   anti-social feeling in the 1960's'" he adds. Back then it was a felony in Alaska to possess marijuana even at home.

Almost without exception, Alas-
115   kan leaders, educators, and lawmen take a tough stance against the use of marijuana by minors. The Anchorage school system, for instance, has rigid rules that include a seven-day suspen-
120   sion for the first offense of possession and 45 days or a semester suspension, whichever is longer, for the first offense of selling. It enforces them vigorously.

125   Although pro-pot advocacy groups in California, Washington, D.C., and elsewhere are promoting liberal marijuana laws patterned after Alaska's, local civic leaders warn that Alaska's
130   experience with its law doesn't necessarily portend similar experiences for other states. This isn't exactly Mid-America they say.

"Alaskans are a very independent
135   lot," explains Katherine Fanning, editor of the *Anchorage Daily News*. "They take this position on marijuana not because they're liberal but because they have enormous concern
140   for individual freedoms and freedom from government interference."

In handing down its 1975 decision, the Alaska supreme court observed, "Our territory and now
145   state has traditionally been the home of people who prize their individuality and who have chosen to settle or to continue living here in order to achieve a measure of control over
150   their own lifestyles which is now virtually unattainable in many of our sister states."

Daniel Hickey, Alaska's chief prosecutor, puts it another way: "In Alaska there's absolutely no consen-
155   sus of opinion on anything."

TEST YOUR READING
COMPREHENSION _____

A. Based on the reading, decide whether the following statements are true or false.

1. Alaskans don't mind the government interfering in their lives.
2. It's legal to grow marijuana in Alaska for personnel use.
3. It's not a crime in Alaska to sell small amounts of marijuana.
4. Alaska is the only state in the nation that permits the smoking of marijuana in public.
5. The decriminalization of backyard marijuana in Alaska has caused problems for the police and prosecutors.
6. The jury decided that Mr. Van Camp intended to sell the marijuana he was growing in his backyard.
7. There are now more problems than ever with children in Alaska smoking pot in school.
8. According to the state's chief prosecutor, Alaskans don't agree about anything.

B. Which of the sentences above best states the main idea of the reading? Circle it.

C. *Vocabulary in Context:* Without using a dictionary, study how the following words or phrases are used in the reading. Work together in pairs to figure out what the words mean.

(3) raw facts
(23) caribou country
(44) wrestled
(55) sinsemilla
(68) granola
(116) take a tough stance
(128) patterned after

D. *Vocabulary 1:* Fill in the blanks with the correct word.

advocacy	discernible	potent	unattainable
circumstantial	felony	rigid	
contended	misdemeanor	seizure	

1. The anonymous tip led to the _____ of the smuggled goods.

2. Penicillin is such a _____ drug that her infection disappeared within days.

3. The prosecutor had to rely on _____ evidence because there were no witnesses to the crime.

4. He _____ that his candidate would make the best president.

5. The union leader was famous for his _____ of unpopular causes.

6. You won't be sent to prison for not putting on your turn signal; it's just a _____ .

7. There was almost no _____ difference between those two white wines.

8. The author's views on the subject were _____ and unyielding.

9. Though his parents were confident he would win the the competition, he felt the grand prize was _____ .

10. Kidnapping is a _____ punishable by life imprisonment.

E. *Vocabulary 2:* Fill in the blanks with the correct word form.

1. **(bulk)** The _____ package was difficult to manage on the crowded bus.

2. **(dispute)** She took the television repairman to small claims court over the _____ bill.

3. **(indict)** The grand jury brought a criminal _____ against the ex-mayor for theft of public funds.

4. **(privacy)** Both husband and wife were such _____ people that we had very little contact with either of them.

5. **(tolerant)** He showed little _____ to alcohol.

6. **(rebel)** Although she was _____ as a teenager, she settled down once she was on her own.

F. *Vocabulary 3:* Write your own sentence using the italicized phrase.

1. The grand jury didn't have to *waste* much *time* arguing over the raw facts in the case.

2. *Almost without exception*, Alaskan leaders, educators, and lawmen take a tough stance against the use of marijuana by minors.

3. Daniel Hickey, Alaska's chief prosecutor, *puts it another way*: "In Alaska there's absolutely no consensus of opinion on anything."

4. *In effect*, the decision legalized home cultivation, smoking, and possession of marijuana.

G. *Vocabulary 4:* These words are often misused. Choose the correct answer and explain your choice.

1. The only question was whether the (**50 pounds, 50-pound**) harvest was for (**personel, personal**) use, which is legal, or whether it was for (**sell, sale, sail**), which isn't.

2. But the court didn't say how much was too much and therein **(lies, lays)** a problem.
3. Nor is the added freedom to puff pot having a discernible **(effect, affect)** on schools, local people say.
4. Local civic leaders warn that Alaska's experience with **(its, it's)** law doesn't necessarily portend similar experiences for **(other, others)** states.

RETELL THE STORY

Use the outline below as a guide to tell the story in class.

- the case of the man who grew 350 marijuana plants
- Alaska's marijuana law
- problems the law causes for prosecutors
- the trial of Mr. Van Camp
- what changes the law has brought about in Alaska
- the state's attitude toward smoking by minors
- Alaskans' independent nature

SPEAK UP

1. *ONE-MINUTE SPEECH:* The article makes the point that Alaskans value individual freedom, including the right to smoke marijuana in the privacy of their homes. There are other ways Americans express their individuality, including:

- dress
- choosing a mate
- lifestyle
- choosing a career
- showing their feelings

Have you observed an example of individual freedom in America? Describe to the class a person or scene that impressed you. Be specific.

2. DEBATE: Do you think Americans have too much individual freedom? Debate one of the topics outlined below.

PRO	CON
1. The institution of marriage has been damaged by liberal divorce laws.	1. Men and women are no longer trapped in unwanted marriages.

2. The stability of the family is threatened by homosexuals.

3. Children are not taught to respect their parents.

2. People should have the right to choose their sexual preference.

3. Children should be encouraged to think for themselves.

TABLE 11-1 Marijuana Use in the United States

AGE GROUP	USED AT LEAST ONCE	USED AT LEAST ONCE IN THE LAST THIRTY DAYS
12–17	27.3%	11.1%
18–25	64.3%	27.5%
26 and older	23.4%	6.7%

Source: National Institute on Drug Abuse, 1982.

Refer to Table 11-1 in answering the following questions.

1. Which age group in America uses marijuana most often? Why do you think this is so?
2. Some people believe marijuana is addictive. Do these figures support their position?

TEST YOUR LISTENING COMPREHENSION

A. Listen to the tape before continuing on. (The Listening Transcript appears on page 135.) Based on the listening, answer the following questions.

1. Will Mr. Evans have to pay $10,000 to the government to get a supply of marijuana cigarettes?
2. What happened to the criminal charges against Mr. Evans?
3. Is marijuana more effective than conventional medicines for Mr. Evans's eye disease?
4. Has New York State legalized marijuana grown and used at home?
5. Do proponents of marijuana say it is a cure for cancer?

B. Listen to the newscast again for these words. Can you guess their meaning from the context?

conventional
therapeutic
enacted
chemotherapy
glaucoma

C. *Listening Carefully:* Your teacher will read the following passage. Fill in the blanks with the missing words.

A District of Columbia man _____ the legal right to use mari-
(1)

juana to keep _____ blind. Roger Evans _____ two
(2)   (3)

years ago for growing _____ supply of marijuana that he
(4)

_____ treat his eye disease. After spending $10,000
(5)

_____ legal fees, Mr. Evans convinced the government that con-
(6)

ventional medicines _____ his sight as well as marijuana. The
(7)

government _____ to supply Mr. Evans with marijuana cigarettes
(8)

and the court _____ charges against him. The treatment
(9)

_____ under a government research project to further study the
(10)

potential of marijuana _____ therapeutic agent.
(11)

INTERVIEW

Use these questions as a guide to interview a classmate. Add questions of your own.

1. Is marijuana used in your country? Who uses it? What happens in your country if you are caught smoking marijuana or using an illicit drug?

 2. Recently a 19-year-old man in West Plains, Missouri was sentenced to twelve years in prison for selling 11 grams of marijuana to undercover agents. If you had been on the jury, what sentence would you have given and why? (acquittal, fine, suspended sentence, probation, drug rehabilitation program, imprisonment, solitary confinement, death penalty)

3. How would you characterize the attitudes of people in your country toward individual freedoms compared with Alaskans? Give specific examples.

12 *Eight Hospitals in City Struck By Doctors*

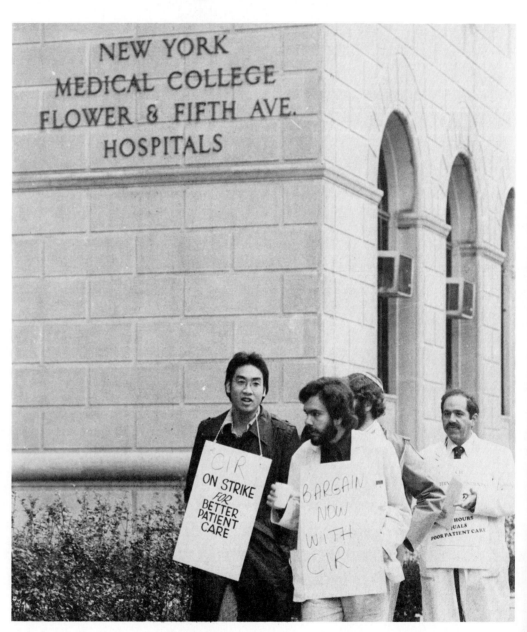

The United States is famous for such medical achievements as organ transplants and artificial heart machines. But there is another side to the American health system: deplorable conditions in some big city public hospitals. Here is the story of a group of doctors who have gone on strike to demand improved patient care.

EIGHT HOSPITALS IN CITY STRUCK BY DOCTORS

"NEEDLESS" DEATHS OF PATIENTS CITED

Improved Staffing Sought

By RONALD SULLIVAN

Nearly 2,000 physicians-in-training struck six municipal and two voluntary hospitals in New York City yesterday morning. They demanded
5 guaranteed minimum staffing levels for nurses, aides, technicians, and other support personnel and an end to what they called chronic shortages of lifesaving medical equipment.
10 "Patients are dying needlessly because of staff and equipment shortages," Dr. Jonathan House shouted to chanting physicians and other hospital employees supporting
15 their demonstration outside Harlem Hospital Center. Only 38 of 222 interns and residents had reported for duty at the hospital.

Hospitals Deny Allegations

20 "The issue is not money," Dr. House said, "but the need to enforce standards of patient care in our contracts."
Dr. House and two other striking
25 physicians later cited specific instances of what they said were needless deaths. In each case officials at the hospitals involved denied the allegations.
30 Defying a state supreme court injunction and a state law barring strikes by public employees, the Committee of Interns and Residents set up picket lines at 7 A.M. The committee is
35 the bargaining agent for interns and

residents completing their medical training in municipal and private vountary hospitals in the city. Dr. House is its president.
40 City officials said patient care was not greatly affected by the strike. Attending physicians worked extended shifts in place of the striking doctors.
45 In an interview, Dr. House said a patient named Rufus Spencer suffered "brain death" unnecessarily last night at Coney Island Hospital when emergency medical equipment failed while
50 physicians were attempting to resuscitate him.
"The man was admitted with hemorrhagic pancreatitis," Dr. House said. "But there was no room for him
55 in the intensive care unit. When he suffered cardiac arrest last night, vital equipment that could have saved his life was not working."

Three Cases at Lincoln Hospital

60 At Lincoln Hospital in the South Bronx two striking physicians said two patients died and the third suffered brain death there recently as a result of negligence.
65 In one case, Dr. Dino Delaportas, chief resident in medicine, said a woman in her late 50's died last July when an alarm on a cardiac monitor

Continued on Page 106, Column 1

did not ring when her heart began to
70 fail.

"They were supposed to be watching her too, but there were not enough nurses to go around," he said. "When I complained about her death,
75 the staff said, 'Please don't go to the press.'"

In one of the two other cases, said Dr. Steve Sowinski, a resident in medicine, Patricio Ruiz, a 74-year-old can-
80 cer victim, died March 6 after going into respiratory arrest on January 24. "The patient died because there was no one to suction him," Dr. Sowinski said, referring to a clogged tube in the
85 patient's throat.

He identified the other patient as 77-year-old Dolores Pujhols, who, he said, suffered brain death unnecessarily on March 7. He said Mrs. Pujhols
90 suffered from meningitis and should have been admitted to the intensive care unit.

"But the I.C.U. was filled," he said, "and she was put in a ward
95 where no one was watching when she underwent respiratory arrest." Mrs. Pujhols is now sustained by a respirator.

"The only way the city will change
100 is to sue it," Dr. Sowinski said. "It's time that patients' families and their attorneys are told when these things happen instead of simply telling them,

'The patient took a turn for the worse.'" 105

Charges Called "Irresponsible"

In each of these cases, however, officials at Lincoln and Coney Island Hospitals denied the allegations after reviewing the records on the patients. 110

A surgeon at Lincoln, speaking for the hospital, called the charges "irresponsible" and said the deaths cited by the striking physicians were not the result of any negligence and "could 115 have happened in any hospital in the country." The surgeon, who asked not to be identified, said that departmental reviews showed that everything possible had been done to save the 120 patients.

Although critics of the municipal hospital system have previously charged that cutbacks in staff and equipment have caused unnecessary 125 deaths, yesterday's allegations were the first in which patients were identified.

Municipal hospital officials said that disclosing the identity of a person 130 who has died in a hospital was "unethical" without the family's permission. They said the unauthorized disclosure of the name of a living patient—such as Mrs. Pujhols, who is on a respira- 135 tor—violated legal canons on patient confidentiality.

TEST YOUR READING
COMPREHENSION _____

    A. Based on the reading, decide whether the following statements are true or false.

1. All hospital interns and residents are on strike in New York City.
2. According to the striking doctors, patients are dying needlessly because of shortages in staff and equipment.
3. The doctors want to be paid more.

4. State law prohibits doctors from going out on strike.
5. The officials at two of the hospitals agreed there was negligence in the deaths of some patients.
6. The strike caused enormous hardships on patients.
7. Medical ethics forbids the disclosure of a patient's name or illness without his consent.
8. Supervisors of the striking doctors are working overtime.

B. Which of the sentences above best states the main idea of the reading? Circle it.

C. *Vocabulary in Context:* Without a dictionary, study how the following words and phrases are used in the reading. Work together in pairs to figure out what the words mean.

(42) extended shifts
(81) respiratory arrest
(83) suction
(109) denied the allegations
(136) legal canons

D. *Vocabulary 1:* Fill in the blanks with the correct word.

barred	defy	injunction	resuscitate	unethical
cutbacks	disclosure	picket	unauthorized	ward

1. Soldiers are taught never to _____ a direct order.

2. The city attorney will appear in court to seek an _____ against the striking bus drivers.

3. Women were _____ from the all-male club.

4. The striking hotel workers held _____ signs and chanted slogans.

5. As hard as they tried to _____ the old man, the paramedics couldn't get his heart pumping.

6. You can find Mrs. Bedick in the maternity _____ on the fifth floor.

7. Because of the fiscal _____, library hours will be shortened again.

8. No _____ person will be allowed in the operating room.

9. The lawyer lost his license because of his _____ conduct.

10. The new law requires candidates to make a full _____ of their net worth.

E. *Vocabulary 2:* Fill in the blanks with the correct word form.

1. **(voluntary)** The mayor called for _____ to help clean up after the flood.

2. **(legal)** A referendum to _____ casino gambling was on the ballot this year.

3. **(fail)** The mother considered herself a _____ as a parent because neither child went to college.

4. **(permit)** The doctor gave him _____ to resume normal activity.

5. **(strike)** Last year the union _____ for higher wages.

6. **(negligence)** The court ordered that the child be taken away from his _____ mother.

7. **(sue)** The jury awarded him $100,000 in his law _____ against his employer.

8. **(previous)** He had been _____ married to a wealthy heiress.

9. **(medicine)** Getting into _____ school is quite competitive.

F. *Vocabulary 3:* Write your own sentence using the italicized phrase.

1. A women *in her late* 50's died last July when an alarm on a cardiac monitor did not ring when her heart began to fail.
2. "They were supposed to be watching her too, but there were not *enough* nurses *to go around*."
3. "The patient *took a turn for the worse*."

G. *Vocabulary 4:* These words are often misused. Choose the correct word and explain your choice.

1. City officials said patient care was not greatly (**affected, effected**) by the strike.
2. Critics have previously charged that cutbacks in staff and (**equipment, equipments**) have caused unnecessary deaths.
3. Departmental reviews showed that everything possible had been (**made, done**) to (**safe, save**) the patients.
4. "It's time that (**patients, patient's, patients'**) families and their attorneys are (**said, told, saying, telling**) when (**this, these**) things happen."

RETELL THE STORY

Use the outline below as a guide to tell the story in class.

- who is on strike
- why they are on strike
- specific allegations made by the doctors
- malfunctioning equipment at Coney Island Hospital
- the three cases at Lincoln Hospital
- response of the officials to these allegations
- ethical obligations of doctors

SPEAK UP

1. *One-Minute Speech:* Choose one of the following topics.
   A. Were you ever treated in a hospital? Briefly describe your experience. Use the following expressions as necessary.

   I was operated on
   I underwent an operation

   B. If you have never been hospitalized, describe a very good (or a very bad) experience you had with a doctor.

2. *Role Play:* Doctor and Patient. The patient is sick and calls the doctor. The doctor must elicit enough information from the patient to decide what should be done. Use the outline and expressions below as a guide.

   PATIENT

   1. Report your temperature and your symptoms.
   2. Tell when the condition started.
   3. Describe other symptoms before this illness.

   DOCTOR

   1. Ask for a description of the pain.
   2. Ask what medication the patient is taking.
   3. Ask if the patient is allergic to anything.
   4. Set up an appointment and give advice.

   EXPRESSIONS

   I feel lousy (crummy, under the weather).
   I feel nauseous (faint, dizzy).
   I'm congested (allergic to . . ., constipated).
   I have a splitting headache (a dry cough, diarrhea).

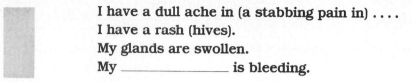

I have a dull ache in (a stabbing pain in) . . . .
I have a rash (hives).
My glands are swollen.
My _____ is bleeding.

TEST YOUR LISTENING COMPREHENSION

A.   Listen to the tape before continuing on. (The Listening Transcript appears on page 135.) Based on the listening, answer the following questions.

1.   How much unnecessary surgery is performed in the United States?
2.   How many lives are lost as a result of this?
3.   What encourages surgery in the United States?
4.   What does the Department of Health want you to do before undergoing nonemergency surgery?
5.   Is more surgery performed in England than in America?
6.   What was the reaction of the American Medical Association to this report?
7.   Does the American Medical Association want mandatory second opinions?

B.   Listen to the newscast again for these words. Can you guess their meaning from the context?

system of hospital reimbursement
proportionately
mandatory

C.   *Listening Carefully:* Your teacher will read aloud the following passage. Fill in the blanks with the missing words.

The Department of Health has released today _____ two
                                                              (1)

nationwide studies _____ that 10 percent _____ surgi-
                            (2)   (3)

cal procedures performed every year _____ United States are
                                              (4)

_____. The report claims that unnecessary surgery causes
        (5)

11,000 _____ and adds 3 billion dollars to the annual cost of
              (6)

health care in America. According to the department's study, an oversup-

ply of surgeons and hospital beds, _____ present system of hospi-

(7)

tal reimbursement, _____ excessive surgery. Proportionately,

(8)

about _____ surgery is performed in the United States

(9)

_____ England.

(10)

INTERVIEW

> Use these questions as a guide to interview a classmate. Add questions of your own.
>
> 1. How does the medical system in your country differ from the American system?
>
>   Is it socialized?
>   Do doctors make house calls?
>   What is the average salary of a doctor?
>   Do people sue doctors for medical malpractice?
>   Do doctors go on strike?
>   Do you need a doctor's prescription to buy drugs?
>   Are the old, the poor, and the unemployed taken care of?
>   Are all workers covered by medical insurance?
>   Are hospital costs prohibitive?
>
> 2. How would you like to see the medical system in your country changed?
>
> 3. Have you had any personal experience with doctors in America? Describe your experience.

13 The Perils of Santa: North Pole Is Safer Than a Large Store

Even for men and women who enjoy working with children, playing Santa for a living does have its drawbacks. This article describes the perils faced by people who spend the month of December with a child on their knee.

THE PERILS OF SANTA: NORTH POLE IS SAFER THAN A LARGE STORE

By JEFFERY H. BIRNBAUM

NEW YORK— Santa Claus isn't always jolly, especially if he works in a department store.

Department-store Santas get uncomfortably hot. They are beaned by precocious children. Their beards get pulled. They aren't paid much. In some places, they are even told not to laugh.

And if they like the job despite all this, a fickle public may turn on them. Take what happened to Bob Horek.

For four years Mr. Horek, also known as Santa Bob, was a fixture on the eighth floor of Macy's department store here. Once a lowly elf in a Detroit store, Mr. Horek had slowly worked his way up to become one of Macy's most popular Santas. Last year the 30-year-old costume designer reached the apex of his Christmas-season career by portraying Santa Claus in Macy's Thanksgiving Day parade. "It was the most exciting day of my life," he says.

Alas, Santa Bob wasn't in this year's parade. In fact, he wasn't a Santa anymore. When he checked in at Macy's last September to make sure he could count on the job again, he learned that the most exciting day of his life had been his downfall.

Unfavorable Reaction

Television viewers, he was informed by Macy officials, had complained about his performance in the parade. "There were letters that said I was an effeminate-looking and -acting Santa," Mr. Horek says. Crushed and embittered by the news, he didn't even ask for his old job back, though Macy's says it would have rehired him—as a store Santa only. ("He was young for the role of parade Santa," a Macy spokesman says.) Mr. Horek says sadly: "I didn't want to give them the satisfaction of saying no. Santa is no longer fun for me. They made him a little bit of a Scrooge."

If Mr. Horek isn't laughing, neither are some rehired Santas. Chortling "ho-ho-ho" is a no-no, according to Western Temporary Services Inc., which recruits Macy's Santas in New York and some 2,000 other Santas across the country. "When you raise your voice, it startles the children," explains Adrian Cohen, the manager of Western's New York branch. And a soft ho-ho-ho is no ho-ho-ho at all.

For every Santa who, like Mr. Horek, drops out, scores are eager to take his place. There are 10,000 Santa Claus jobs in the U.S., and the number of applications far exceeds the supply. Many of the applicants are unemployed actors. Many others simply like Christmas and children so much that they take time out from their regular work to promote the Christmas spirit.

In the New York area Mr. Cohen begins interviewing prospective Santas in August, ultimately choosing

Continued on Page 114, Column 1

75 about 80 from a field of nearly 600. Macy's takes up to 22 of these. Basically, Mr. Cohen looks for someone with a kind heart and thick skin. He notes that "there are easier ways to 80 earn money" than spending a month as Santa Claus.

Minority Clauses

Santa candidates needn't be plump or old or even male. Macy's has 85 long had at least one female Santa every year—dressed in full beard. The main qualification is a deep voice. This year Macy's has one woman Santa: 98-pound, five-foot two-inch 90 Albina Vurro, who says she is "just tickled pink" with her new job.

Western also hires Santas of various ethnic and racial backgrounds. It isn't always easy to find them, though. 95 When the New York office this year sent circulars to such groups as the Negro Actors Guild of America and the Association of Hispanic Arts, no one responded. Ads in actors' trade 100 publications were more successful.

Marshall Field's downtown Chicago department store, which hasn't hired its Santas through Western, has never had a nonwhite Santa. "We 105 haven't had any apply," says Homer Sharp, a vice-president. Says Mr. Cohen: "We are conditioned, unfortunately, that we live in a white man's world."

110 This prejudice carries over to Santa's visitors. "If parents insist, we do direct the children to the 'right' ethnic Santa," says Jean McFaddin, Macy's special-promotions director. 115 Macy's this year has black Santas and Santas who know sign-language greetings for deaf children. If confronted by a disgruntled parent or child, Western's nonwhite Santas are told to just 120 say that Santa comes in all colors and quickly move the child on.

Although some Santas just jump into a suit and improvise, Western's recruits are tutored in the nuances of

the trade. "This is really an expert's 125 business," Mr. Cohen says. "We aren't street Santas; we're professionals."

At a recent half-day session here, two dozen mostly scrawny Santas were lectured on the subtleties of 130 proper pillow placement and learned some do's and don'ts. Don't eat onions at lunch. Do wash your beard in Woolite—frequently. Avoid being seen with other Santas in public. Even 135 if kicked in the shin, never make un-Santa-like remarks.

There are plenty of reasons for Santas to turn grumpy. One hazard is the backache, or "Santa sacroiliac," 140 caused by repeated lifting of lads to laps. And there is always the over-excited tot who inflicts "diaper rash of the knee." Mr. Cohen advises: "If you get the 'royal christening,' call over 145 your elf immediately."

One longtime Santa in Dayton's department store in Minneapolis got a christening he won't forget. The Santa, who works off-season as an 150 investment analyst and prefers to remain anonymous, once greeted two "parents" who persuaded him to pose with their fully clothed chimpanzee for a photo. Everything went smoothly 155 until the flashbulb went off, and then the chimp went ape. Ripping off Santa's beard and losing control of its bodily functions, the animal shrieked almost as loudly as the frightened elf 160 behind the camera. The line had to be closed off for nearly an hour for a thorough scrubbing.

A Truck Accident

Another Santa, in Denver some 165 years ago, was approached by a boy who didn't get what he wanted for Christmas. The boy promptly crowned Santa with a metal toy truck. Santa needed stitches. 170

Youngsters' requests can be surprising. At a New York Gimbels store, Santa Sam Cardona asked a teenage boy what he wanted for Christmas. "I

175 want a girl," the boy answered. "What do you want a girl for?" the startled Santa asked. "Santa, you know why," was the response.

Oldsters, too, can be difficult. A 180 New York grandfather offered his grandson $5 to pull off Santa's beard. The wily Mr. Claus foiled the plan by screaming in mock pain at the first tug.

185   **Feeding the Reindeer**

Most of Western's Santas take a breather—or, as they say, "go feed the reindeer"—every couple of hours. In some places, though, Santas aren't given the rest they need, so they 190 sometimes suffer "Santa burnout." One such victim of overwork was Kevin McClosky, 30, a free-lance artist, who a few years ago lost his ability to communicate outside his job. "I 195 would try to say something to my wife," he recalls, "and all I could get out was, 'What is your name?'" He recovered and now he is a Santa at Macy's.   200

For all their complaints, most Santas seem to love their jobs. "By the time Christmas finally comes, I swear I'll never do it again," says one Santa. "But by August I'm singing 'Jingle Bells.'"   205

TEST YOUR READING COMPREHENSION

A.   Based on the reading, decide whether the following statements are true or false.

1. Working as a department store Santa can be a difficult job.
2. Macy's fired one Santa from the Thanksgiving Day parade because he was too old.
3. There is a shortage of people who want to work as a Santa.
4. Western Temporary Services teaches a short course on how to be a Santa.
5. One Santa in Minneapolis was attacked by a chimpanzee.
6. A boy in Denver gave back a toy truck he didn't like.
7. You don't have to be a plump white male to work as a Santa.
8. Santa burnout is caused by overwork.

B.   Which of the sentences above best states the main idea of the reading? Circle it.

C.   *Vocabulary in Context:* Without using a dictionary, study how the following words or phrases are used in the reading. Work together in pairs to figure out what the words mean.

(5) beaned
(14) was a fixture
(21) the apex of
(50) a Scrooge
(52) chortling
(91) tickled pink

(157) went ape
(168) crowned
(183) in mock pain
(184) tug
(191) burnout

D. *Vocabulary 1:* Fill in the blanks with the correct word.

embittered	free-lance	improvised	plump	shrieked
fickle	grumpy	lap	precocious	stitches

1. His five-year old child was so _____ that she could read the newspaper and use a computer.

2. Every week the _____ boy fell in love with a different girl.

3. Members of the union felt _____ toward their employer after the six-month strike.

4. After a year in America, she had gained twenty pounds and looked quite _____.

5. The actress skillfully _____ when she forgot her lines.

6. Whenever he didn't get enough sleep, he was _____ and would yell at the children.

7. Before eating, spread the napkin on your _____.

8. When the acceptance letter came, she _____ with joy.

9. He cut himself so badly that he needed eight _____.

10. She was a _____ photographer whose pictures often appeared in fashion magazines.

E. *Vocabulary 2:* Fill in the blanks with the correct word form.

1. (startle)   How _____ he was when she rushed into the room unannounced!

2. (prospect)   Her parents considered all of her dates _____ sons-in-laws.

3. (ultimate)   He was sure that the jury would _____ find him innocent.

4. (crush)   When the young man was turned down for the job, he felt so _____ that he couldn't bear to tell his wife.

5. (promote)   After two years on the job, she received a _____ and a raise.

6. **(expert)**   He was hired for his _____ in the field of weather forecasting.

F.   *Vocabulary 3:* **Write your own sentence using the italicized phrase.**

1. Mr. Horek had slowly *worked his way up* to become one of Macy's most popular Santas.
2. And if they like the job despite all this, a fickle public may *turn on them.*
3. Many others simply like Christmas and children so much that they *take time out* from their regular work to promote the Christmas spirit.
4. Mr. Cohen looks for someone with a kind heart and *a thick skin.*

G.   *Vocabulary 4:* **These words are often confused. Choose the correct answer and explain your choice.**

1. For four years Mr. Horek, also known as Santa Bob, was a fixture (**in, on**) the eighth floor of Macy's department store here.
2. (**The, 0**) last year the (**30 year old, 30-year-old**) costume designer reached the apex of his career.
3. In fact, he wasn't a Santa (**anymore, no more**).
4. "He was young for the (**rule, role, roll**) of parade Santa," a Macy spokesman says.
5. The number of applications far (**exceed, exceeds**) the supply.
6. This year Macy's has one woman Santa: 98-pound, (**five-feet, five-foot**) two-inch Albina Vurro.
7. Avoid (**to be, been, being**) seen with other Santas in public.

RETELL THE STORY

Use the outline below as a guide to tell the story in class.

- being a Santa isn't always jolly
- Mr. Horek's experience at Macy's
- qualifications needed to be a Santa
- minority clauses
- do's and don't's for Santas
- reasons for Santas to turn grumpy (chimpanzee story and the toy truck)
- surprising requests
- the grandfather's five-dollar bet
- "Santa burnout"
- some Santas still love their jobs

SPEAK UP

1. **ONE-MINUTE SPEECH:** Describe your present job in detail: your employer, your position and responsibilities, and the advantages and disadvantages of the job. If you are not working, describe your ideal job.

2. **DESCRIPTION:** How does one go about getting a job in your country? Pick a specific field and give detailed steps.

3. **ROLE PLAY:** *Employer and Job Seeker.*

Job Seeker: Find a job that interests you in the help wanted ads in the newspaper. Be prepared to outline your experience, your education, and your abilities to the prospective employer. Ask questions about the job: hours, salary, benefits, and opportunities for advancement.

Employer: Question the job seeker about his or her experience and capabilities. Explain the job requirements. Use the expressions below.

I have a background in . . . .

I enjoy working with . . . .

Have you had any experience in . . .?

Would you be willing to (work overtime, start next week, relocate)?

TABLE 13-1 What Americans Want Most From Their Jobs (listed in order of importance)

1.	Important work that gives a feeling of accomplishment
2.	High income
3.	Chance for advancement
4.	No danger of being fired
5.	Short working hours, a lot of free time

Source: adapted from surveys taken by the National Opinion Research Center, University of Chicago

Refer to Table 13-1 in answering the following questions.

1. How would you rate the importance of these five factors?

TEST YOUR LISTENING COMPREHENSION

A. Listen to the tape before continuing on. (The Listening Transcript appears on page 136.) Based on the listening, answer the following questions.

1. Who was arrested?
2. What is the goal of the "Project Jobs" operation?
3. Was the head of the program pleased with the raid?
4. What were the conclusions of the President's Commission on Immigration and Refugee Policy?
5. How many undocumented workers are there in the U.S.?

6. Why don't Americans want these jobs?

B. Listen to the newscast again for these words. Can you guess their meaning from the context?

undocumented
goal
unqualified success
dead-end
demeaning

C. *Listening Carefully:* **Your teacher will read the following passage. Fill in the blanks with the missing words.**

However, the _____ Commission on Immigration and Refugee
           (1)

Policy issued _____ last week that concluded that there is
           (2)

_____ that illegal aliens _____ jobs from American
   (3)   (4)

workers. _____ there are as many as 6 _____ undocu-
        (5)   (6)

mented aliens _____ United States, the Commission found that
        (7)

_____ largely unskilled laborers _____ jobs that
   (8)   (9)
Americans want.

INTERVIEW

Use these questions as a guide to interview a classmate. Add questions of your own.

1. Is there a job you have done which you would never want to do again? Explain.
2. Which professions are considered prestigious in your country? Which jobs are considered "low status"? What are they and why? (soldier, lawyer, politician, psychiatrist, priest, firefighter, actor, waiter, taxi driver, police officer, bartender, butcher)
3. Do you work in a competitive field? Describe the situation for people who want to enter the field.
4. In a recent poll, two-thirds of American workers said that they would continue working on their job even if they had enough money to live comfortably. What would you do if you were financially independent?

14 *The Only Gentleman*

The American author Mark Twain (1835–1910) was a master of irony. His book Huckleberry Finn, *first published in 1884, generated considerable controversy about its depiction of white and black Americans living along the Mississippi River in the years before slavery was outlawed. Here Russell Baker, an editorial columnist for the* New York Times *and a master of irony himself, examines the latest dispute about this classic of American fiction.*

THE ONLY GENTLEMAN

By RUSSELL BAKER

The question of what books are fit for young eyes has arisen again in the Washington suburbs, where authorities are arguing whether the Mark Twain Intermediate School of Fairfax County should drop Mark Twain's *Huckleberry Finn,* from the curriculum. My immediate question is, what's it doing in the curriculum in the first place?

It's a dreadful disservice to Mark Twain for teachers to push *Huckleberry Finn* on seventh-, eighth-, and ninth-graders. I had it forced on me in eleventh grade and, after the hair-raising opening passages about Huck's whisky-besotted "Pap," found it tedious in the extreme. Thereafter I avoided it for years. It had been poisoned for me by schoolteachers who drove me to it before I was equipped to enjoy it.

I had similar experiences with Shakespeare (*As You Like It* and *Macbeth*), George Eliot (*Silas Marner*), Charles Dickens (*A Tale of Two Cities*), and Herman Melville (*Moby Dick*). Schoolteachers seemed determined to persuade me that "classic" was a synonym for "narcotic."

Ever since, it's been my aim to place severe restrictions on teachers' power to assign great books. Under my system any teacher caught assigning Dickens to a person under the age of 25 would be sentenced to teach summer school at half pay.

Punishment would be harsher for assigning *Moby Dick,* a book accessible only to people old enough to know what it is to rail at God about the inevitability of death.

Huckleberry Finn can be partly enjoyed after the age of 25, but for fullest benefit it probably shouldn't be read before age 35 and even then only if the reader has had a broad experience of American society.

Unfortunately, this sensible reason for pruning the school curriculum has not been advanced in Fairfax County's case for dropping *Huckleberry Finn.* Instead of pointing out that assigning the book to adolescents damages Mark Twain, the authorities argue that Mark Twain damages the students.

John H. Wallace, one of the school's administrators, makes the case in *The Washington Post.* The book "uses the pejorative term 'nigger' profusely." (It does.) "It speaks of black Americans with implications that they are not honest, they are not as intelligent as whites, and they are not human."

While this is meant to be satirical, and is, Mr. Wallace concedes, it also "ridicules blacks," is "extremely difficult for black youngsters to handle," and therefore subjects them to "mental cruelty, harassment, and outright racial intimidation."

I suppose a black youngster of 12, 13, or 14 might very well suffer the anguish Mr. Wallace describes, and even white youngsters of that age might misread Mark Twain as outra-

Continued on Page 122, Column 1

geously as Mr. Wallace has in thinking
80 the book is about the dishonesty,
dumbness, and inhumanity of blacks.
This is the kind of risk you invite when
you assign books of some subtlety to
youngsters mentally unprepared to
85 enjoy them.

Mr. Wallace thinks Mark Twain
aimed only to be "satirical," but only
in the loosest sense can *Huckleberry
Finn* be called a satire. It is the darkest
90 of visions of American society, and it
isn't satire that makes it a triumph,
but an irony full of pessimism about
the human race and particularly its
white American members.

95 Irony is the subtlest of artistic
devices, and one of the hardest for
youngsters to grasp. It requires
enough experience of life to enable
you to perceive the difference
100 between the world as it is and the
world as it is supposed to be. Many
adults have trouble seeing that the
world Huck and Jim traverse along
the Mississippi is not a boyhood
adventure land out of Disney, but a 105
real landscape swarming with native
monsters.

The people they encounter are
drunkards, murderers, bullies, swin-
dlers, lynchers, thieves, liars, frauds, 110
child abusers, numbskulls, hypo-
crites, windbags, and traders in
human flesh. All are white. The one
man of honor in this phantasmagoria
is black Jim, the runaway slave—"Nig- 115
ger Jim," as Twain called him to
emphasize the irony of a society in
which the only true gentleman was
held beneath contempt.

You can see why a black child 120
nowadays, when "nigger" is such a
taboo word that even full-blooded rac-
ists are too delicate to use it, might
cringe and hurt too much to understand what Twain was really up to. It 125
takes a lot of education and a lot of
living to grasp these ironies and smile,
which is why adolescents shouldn't be
subjected to *Huckleberry Finn.*

TEST YOUR READING COMPREHENSION

A. **Based on the reading, decide whether the following statements are true or false.**

1. Russell Baker agrees that Mark Twain's *Huckleberry Finn* should be dropped from the school curriculum, but not because it might disturb young children.
2. According to Russell Baker, the book should be dropped because it uses the word "nigger."
3. Mr. Baker believes students should not read classics until they are old enough to appreciate them.
4. Mr. Baker feels that John Wallace, one of the school administrators, misunderstood *Huckleberry Finn.*
5. Mr. Wallace feels that the book is unfair to white people.
6. The only gentleman in *Huckleberry Finn* is Jim, the runaway slave.
7. Mark Twain praised American society in *Huckleberry Finn.*
8. According to Mr. Baker, irony is easy for youngsters to understand.

B. **Which of the sentences above best states the main idea of the reading? Circle it.**

C. *Vocabulary in Context:* Without a dictionary, study how the following words and phrases are used in the reading. Work together in pairs to figure out what the words mean.

(7) curriculum
(11) a dreadful disservice
(15) hair-raising
(29) a synonym for "narcotic"
(50) pruning
(119) held beneath contempt

D. *Vocabulary 1:* Fill in the blanks with the correct word.

accessible	grasp	narcotics	swarming
anguish	harsh	pejorative	taboo
conceded	inevitable	profusely	tedious
cringed			

1. It was _____ work typing reports all day long.

2. The heroin pusher was arrested by agents from the _____ squad.

3. A 30-year prison term for smoking marijuana is too _____ .

4. A successful politician makes himself _____ to the voters.

5. After he found her dog, she thanked him _____ .

6. In the debate the senator _____ that a small tax increase might be necessary.

7. Incest is _____ in most societies.

8. He _____ with fear when his father raised his hand in anger.

9. His _____ over the accident subsided when he realized his son would recover.

10. He described his ex-wife in such _____ terms!

11. Having failed to attend class all semester, it was _____ that he flunk the final exam.

12. No matter how long he studied, he couldn't _____ the concept.

13. The store was _____ with shoppers for the Election Day sale.

E. *Vocabulary 2:* Fill in the blanks with the correct word form.

1. **(perceive)**   His _____ of her was blinded by love.

2. **(irony)**   How _____ it would be if she returned to her ex-husband!

3. **(harassment)**   She complained of being sexually _____ by her boss.

4. **(cruel)**   _____ to animals should be severely punished.

5. **(intimidate)**   She felt too _____ to talk back to her father.

6. **(outrage)**   It is _____ how much they charge you to park your car in the city!

7. **(poison)**   Don't eat those berries; they're _____ .

8. **(dread)**   It's _____ the way that man abuses his horse!

9. **(satire)**   The _____ show was banned because it made fun of the government.

F. *Vocabulary 3:* Write your own sentence using the italicized phrase.

1. I had it *forced on* me in the eleventh grade.
2. It had been poisoned for me by schoolteachers who *drove me to* it before I was equipped to enjoy it.
3. You can see why a black child might cringe and hurt too much to understand what Twain *was* really *up to.*
4. Irony is *the subtlest of* artistic devices, and one of the hardest for youngsters to grasp.
5. It takes a lot of education and a lot of living to grasp these ironies and smile, which is why adolescents shouldn't *be subjected to* "Huckleberry Finn."

G. *Vocabulary 4:* Answer these questions by choosing the correct word from the right-hand column.

What would you call someone

1. who drinks whiskey all day long?   a. a hypocrite
2. who gets his way by intimidation?   b. a swindler
3. who sells a home he doesn't own?   c. a drunkard
4. who hangs someone without a lawful trial?   d. a windbag
5. who keeps making the same mistakes?   e. a numbskull

6. who falsely makes himself appear to be virtuous or good?
7. who talks endlessly but says nothing?

f. a bully
g. a lyncher

RETELL THE STORY

Use the outline below as a guide to tell the story in class.

- what controversy surrounds *Huckleberry Finn* at the Mark Twain Intermediate School
- Russell Baker's reason for not reading classics in school
- his "punishment" for teachers assigning classics
- the school's reasons for dropping *Huckleberry Finn*
- how the school misunderstood the book
- the true meaning of *Huckleberry Finn*

SPEAK UP

1. ONE-MINUTE SPEECH: Choose one of the following topics.
   A. Has there recently been a controversy in your country about a movie, a book, a television show, or a newspaper article? Tell the class what, where, when, and why.
   B. Describe your reaction to a classic that was forced upon you in school. How old were you at the time? Has your opinion of the book changed now that you are older?
2. DEBATE: Should newspapers be allowed to print articles critical of the government?

PRO	CON
1. There is no such thing as a free country without a free press.	1. The government cannot function properly if it is constantly attacked in the press.
2. The government should not be allowed to hide its mistakes from the people.	2. Some crucial information must be kept from foreign governments.
3. Most government secrets are a cover-up for official corruption.	3. Writing about corruption does not solve the problem. A country should not air its dirty linen in public.

TABLE 14-1 Some Censored Books

BOOK/AUTHOR	COUNTRY/DATE	REASON
Analects Confucius	China 250 B.C.	first ruler of T'sin dynasty burned all books on Confucius' teachings
The Koran	Switzerland 1542	confiscated by Basel authorities
Huckleberry Finn Clemens, Samuel	Concord, Mass. U.S.A. 1885	called "trash" and "suitable only for slums," the book was banned
The Bible	Russia 1926	only anti-religious books were authorized; was banned in libraries
Alice's Adventures in Wonderland Carroll, Lewis	China 1931	banned on the grounds that animals should not use human language
The Merchant of Venice Shakespeare, William	Buffalo, N.Y. 1931	eliminated from schools because it was declared to be anti-Semitic
Tropic of Cancer Miller, Henry	Greece 1970	after this work was ruled obscene, all copies were ordered destroyed

Refer to Table 14-1 in answering the following questions.

1. Does it surprise you that any of these books has been banned?
2. Do you believe any of these reasons justifies the banning of a book?

TEST YOUR LISTENING COMPREHENSION

A. Listen to the tape before continuing on. (The Listening Transcript appears on page 136.) Based on the listening, answer the following questions.

1. What is the Acme Drug Company going to do?
2. Why?
3. How many followers does the Church of the Lord have?
4. What is the church fighting against?
5. If the Acme Drug Company didn't comply, what would the Church of the Lord do?
6. What did five high school students do?
7. What is Stephen Pico's reason?
8. What did the school board say?

B. Listen to the newscast again for these words. Can you guess their meaning from the context?

sponsors
withdraw

offensive
boycott
suit
anti-Semitic
filthy

C. *Listening Carefully:* Your teacher will read aloud the following passage. Fill in the blanks with the missing words.

One of television's largest _____ , the Acme Drug Company,
(1)

_____ today to withdraw _____ from four shows that a
(2)   (3)

church group _____ to be offensive. The Church of the Lord,
(4)

headquartered in Abilene, Texas, _____ "clean-up television"
(5)

campaign which has attracted _____ followers in the United
(6)

States and Canada. The church _____ to boycott products
(7)

sold by Acme Drug Company _____ company stopped
(8)

advertising _____ television shows _____ sex and
(9)   (10)

violence.

INTERVIEW

Use these questions as a guide to interview your classmates. Add questions of your own.

1. Censorship is the practice of restricting the availability of books, periodicals, plays, films, or works of art that the government believes to be immoral or undesirable. Describe how censorship works in your country using the following questions as a guide.

   What type of books are kept out of bookstores?
   Do newspapers print articles critical of the government?
   Are some movies banned?
   Are there restrictions placed on the themes or the type of art produced by painters, playwrights, and musicians?

Does the government control what appears on television?

2. How do people get around censorship laws in your country?
3. Do you think censorship should be stricter or less strict? Or removed entirely? What, if anything, should be censored?

sex films
violent television shows
magazines like *Playboy*
newspaper articles ridiculing the president
history textbooks
books critical of religion
reports on government wrongdoing

Give specific reasons why you believe any of these should be censored.

Appendix I: Listening Transcripts

LISTENING TRANSCRIPT
FOR CHAPTER 1 _____

Good morning. And here's the latest news at eight o'clock.

The latest figures from the United States Immigration and Naturalization Service show that _well over_ one million immigrants are now _arriving in_ America every year. This is _the highest_ number of newcomers _to the United States_ since the mass migration of Europeans _at the_ turn of the century.

The new immigrants no longer come mainly from Europe. According to the official _government_ estimate, _the greatest_ source of _immigrants_ to America is now Asia, _followed by_ Latin America. Forty-two percent of the new immigrants come from Asia while 39 percent come from Latin America. Only 13 percent of the recent immigration to America is now from Europe.

Although the United States now accepts twice as many foreigners as all other nations combined, Congress is studying several proposals to limit immigration, including a new ceiling of about 450,000 immigrants a year. It is less clear what Congress will do about the problem of illegal immigrants. An estimated 500,000 to one million persons enter the United States illegally every year. Several congressmen have introduced legislation that would make it illegal for employers to knowingly hire an illegal alien. A company would face a heavy fine if convicted of hiring a person without proper papers. Many business groups and civil rights leaders oppose this proposal because they fear it would lead to wholesale discrimination against Hispanics and other recent immigrants.

LISTENING TRANSCRIPT
FOR CHAPTER 2 _____

Good evening and here is the news at six o'clock.

A government task force _has issued_ a report on the hazards of drunk driving. _According to the_ report, half of the 50,000 highway _deaths_ last year involved intoxicated drivers. Annually, drunk drivers cause 80,000 accidents, 750,000 serious injuries, and 5 *billion* dollars in economic *losses*. Federal studies show that on weekend nights *one out of* ten motorists is intoxicated but just *one in* 2,000 is arrested. The *government has* proposed to *strengthen* laws against drunk driving.

In a related story, a Manhattan man has been charged with manslaughter and drunken driving as a result of a collision on the Queensboro Bridge. The two women in his sports car were killed. He was seriously injured and the two men in the second vehicle, a tractor-trailer truck, suffered minor injuries. The three survivors were taken to Saint Vincent's Hospital for treatment. The two female victims were not immediately identified. The accident temporarily closed all but one eastbound lane on the bridge.

And here at 6:05 is the latest traffic report. There is heavy congestion on the Long Island Expressway in both directions. There are tie-ups on all of the westbound crossings to New Jersey. Due to an overturned vehicle in the right lane, traffic is bumper to bumper through the Holland Tunnel. And on the George Washington Bridge, traffic is at a standstill because of a stalled commuter bus. To avoid getting stuck in this traffic, take the Lincoln Tunnel where traffic is moving.

LISTENING TRANSCRIPT FOR CHAPTER 3

Good evening. This is the five o'clock news.

In the top story today, a black couple *has been granted* a judgment for $30,000 *against a* landlord in Westchester, New York, *the largest* award ever *in a* housing discrimination case. Mr. Thorton Williams, a computer programmer for IBM, began looking *for an* apartment in Westchester after his company transferred him from Chicago. According to the testimony *at the* trial, Mr. Williams and his wife visited two buildings in White Plains *owned by the* defendant, Richard Wexler. Although both apartments displayed "Apartment for Rent" signs, the Williams family *was told by* Mr. Wexler that the apartments *had just been* rented. They then brought *suit* in federal court under the Fair Housing Act that prohibits discrimination *in the sale* or rental of housing. A jury of six persons deliberated two hours before reaching its verdict. The attorney for Mr. Wexler says an appeal is planned.

And in Memphis, Tennessee, today thousands of supporters of the late Reverend Martin Luther King, Jr., have gathered to commemorate the anniversary of his death. On April 4, 1968, Dr. King, the civil rights activist and Nobel Peace Prize winner, preached his last sermon in the Mason Temple Church of God a few hours before he was assassinated while standing on the balcony of his motel. A brief period of meditation will be held tomorrow at the church followed by a march through downtown Memphis. The march is sponsored by the American Federation of State, County, and Municipal

Employees, the union representing the striking garbagemen whose cause led Dr. King to come to Memphis in 1968.

LISTENING TRANSCRIPT
FOR CHAPTER 4

Good afternoon. And here's the latest news at three o'clock.

Voters in California will go *to the polls* next week to vote on Proposition 10, a proposal to require no-smoking areas *in all enclosed* public places. Proposition 10 *would also* require employers to establish no-smoking areas *if their* employees requested it. Violators of the proposed law *could be fined* $15.00. A similar proposition *was rejected* two years ago after tobacco companies *spent* $6.3 million *on an* advertising campaign *against it.*

In a related story, a recent report published in the New England Journal of Medicine provided evidence that working in a roomful of smokers is harmful to nonsmokers. The University of California studied the effects of second-hand smoke on over 2,000 middle-aged men and women. Their report concluded that working next to a person who smokes causes the same lung damage as smoking eleven cigarettes a day.

Next Thursday an estimated 16 million smokers will try not to light up during the annual Great American Smokeout sponsored by the American Cancer Society. Smokers in cities and towns all across America will try to go without smoking for as many hours as they can on Thursday and approximately one million of them will quit for good. In Sarasota, Florida, the police and the fire departments have a bet on which department will have more members quit. And in Solvang, California, officials are trying to get the whole town to quit. A recent government study indicates that nearly 34 million Americans have already quit smoking.

LISTENING TRANSCRIPT
FOR CHAPTER 5

Good morning and here's the news at eight o'clock.

The General Motors Corporation announced today that it *plans* to recall 6.4 million mid-size cars *built* between 1978 and 1981. This is *the second biggest* safety recall on record. G.M. said that car owners *will receive written* notification to bring *their cars* to G.M. dealers for replacement of two rear suspension bolts. If the bolts break, the rear axle *can become detached* from the car and cause *a loss of* control. According to G.M., 27 accidents and 22 *injuries* have resulted from this defect. The bolts *will be replaced* without charge to the owners.

And in a broad campaign to get ineffective drugs off the market, the Health Research Group has published a new book entitled "Pills That Don't Work." According to Dr. Sidney Wolfe, director of the Public Citizens Health Research Group, Americans spent 297 billion dollars on health care last year, some of that money on useless and even dangerous drugs. Dr. Wolfe believes that increased consumer awareness about prescription drugs is changing the doctor–patient relationship for the better.

LISTENING TRANSCRIPT FOR CHAPTER 6

Good evening and here's the news at five o'clock.

According to the figures *just published* by the United States Department of Agriculture, the diet *of the* average American *has changed* considerably in the past twenty years. Americans *are now eating* more chicken, fish, and seafood but less lamb and veal. Cheese *has become a* favorite American food with consumption up 71 percent in the past two decades. Calorie-conscious Americans are consuming *less whole* milk and butter *than ever* before. *On the* other hand, the use of sugar *and other* sweeteners has climbed sharply, largely because *of a* 175 percent increase in soft drink consumption. The figures also show that the average American *eats* eighteen pounds of ice cream *a year.*

Although the American diet has changed, the average American family still spends less than 20 percent of its disposable income on food, less than almost any other country in the world.

And in a related story, the results of a Gallop poll on the foods Americans like the least were released today. Snails topped the list as the most unappealing food for Americans; 43 percent of those questioned said they would never eat snails. Brains came in a close second, rejected by 41 percent of those polled. Only 5 percent of the respondents said they would never eat liver.

LISTENING TRANSCRIPT FOR CHAPTER 7

Good morning and here's the news at ten o'clock.

According *to a new* study by the United States Department of Labor, the number of working women in America *has risen* 95 percent *over the past* two decades, and many of the jobs now *filled* by women were once largely *held* by men. In several *major* categories, including insurance adjusters, real-estate brokers, and production-line assemblers, women now outnumber men, *a complete reversal* from the proportion twenty years ago. Nearly 50 percent of *the nation's* bus drivers and bartenders are now women, *compared with* 10 percent twenty years ago.

The Labor Department study reported a sharp increase in female employment in the professions as well. Women now make up 14 percent of the legal profession. And women account for more than one doctor in five. The report added that only 4 percent of engineers are women.

The Labor Department figures also showed that gains in female employment were not matched by increases in salaries. The median annual salary of a woman working full time was only 60 percent of the average male salary. The House of Representatives will hold hearings this fall to study proposals to enforce the Equal Pay Act of 1963, which guarantees women the right to equal pay for equal work.

LISTENING TRANSCRIPT FOR CHAPTER 8

Good evening and here's the news at eight o'clock.

As the temperature dropped to the twenties in the New York City metropolitan area yesterday, thousands of tenants called the city's heat emergency center to complain of little or no heat in their apartments. Yesterday over four thousand complaints were received. If a landlord fails to provide adequate heat, he can now receive a fine of up to $250 a day. The 24-hour heat emergency number to call with complaints is 960-4800.

And in a related story, a landlord who pleaded guilty to deliberately withholding heat from his tenants was *sentenced to* spend four nights *in an* emergency tenant shelter *or else* go to jail. Judge Randolph Carr *told the* landlord, John Lawson, *that a* stay in the shelter, *which has been furnished* with cots and blankets for families with heatless apartments, *would give* him an opportunity to meet many of the residents in his community *who had been forced* to obtain emergency housing because landlords did not provide sufficient heat. Mr. Lawson, *who was also fined* $2,000 by Judge Carr, was brought into court in handcuffs when he *failed to* answer several summonses *served on* his building.

LISTENING TRANSCRIPT FOR CHAPTER 9

Good morning and here's the news at nine o'clock.

According *to a* United Nations study released today, a college education is *more easily* attained *in the* United States *than in any other major* nation. The U.N. report showed that fifty-two *out of every* one thousand Americans attended a college or university this year. The proportion of *Americans* enrolled in colleges and universities was 300 percent *higher than in* Great Britain and 160 percent *higher than in the* Soviet Union. The report said that 12.3 *million* students, *including a* record high of 300,000 *foreign* students, attended American colleges this year. Also, there are more blacks and women in colleges than ever before. Nine percent of today's undergrads are black and 52 percent are women.

As more students find they need to work while attending school, part-time enrollment has grown. Steep rises in tuition and cuts in federal aid may turn more students away from college in the future.

As a result, many universities are trying to recruit foreign students to make up for the potential drop in American students. Right now foreign students account for nearly 3 percent of the college population, and experts predict that in the near future foreign students will represent 10 percent of the college population. This influx of foreign students is bringing in an additional 1.5 billion dollars a year to the American economy.

LISTENING TRANSCRIPT FOR CHAPTER 10

Good morning and here's the news at seven o'clock.

In a report issued today the President's Commission on Foreign Language and International Studies strongly criticized America's "scandalous incompetence" in foreign languages. The commission estimated that there are 100,000 English-speaking Japanese business representatives in the United States, but fewer than 900 Americans in Japan with a working knowledge of Japanese. According to the commission, the deficit in the U.S. balance of trade is due in part to the fact that Americans don't speak foreign languages well enough to persuade others to buy our goods and services.

Only 15 percent of American high school students now study a foreign language, and only one in twenty studies French, German, or Russian beyond the second year. The commission also reported that only 8 percent of American colleges and universities now require a foreign language for admission.

And in Paris *the French* government *has* banned the use of 127 English words *in order to* protect *the French* language *from* foreign intruders. Public establishments *will be fined* 50 francs (about 7 dollars) every time they use one of the *forbidden terms*. Words *on the list* include "pay TV," "jet," "jogging," and "hot dog."

LISTENING TRANSCRIPT
FOR CHAPTER 11

Good evening and here's the news at nine o'clock.

A District of Columbia man *has finally won* the legal right to use marijuana to keep *from going* blind. Roger Evans *was arrested* two years ago for growing *his own* supply of marijuana that he *used to* treat his eye disease. After spending $10,000 *in* legal fees, Mr. Evans convinced the government that conventional medicines *could not save* his sight as well as marijuana. The government *has now agreed* to supply Mr. Evans with marijuana cigarettes and the court *dismissed the* charges against him. The treatment *is being provided* under a government research project to further study the potential of marijuana *as a* therapeutic agent.

The New York State Legislature today passed a bill to allow the medical use of marijuana in controlled research programs. Twenty-three other states have enacted similar measures in recent years. Proponents of marijuana say it eliminates nausea and lack of appetite in cancer patients undergoing chemotherapy and may also be useful against glaucoma, alcoholism, and other diseases. Critics of the medical use of marijuana contend it is a dangerous drug that is already too widely available. The United States Food and Drug Administration has refused to approve marijuana as a prescription drug until further laboratory testing is completed.

LISTENING TRANSCRIPT
FOR CHAPTER 12

Good evening and here's the news at six o'clock.

The Department of Health has released today *the results of* two nationwide studies *which indicate that* 10 percent *of the* surgical procedures performed every year *in the* United States are *unnecessary*. The report claims that unnecessary surgery causes 11,000 *deaths per year* and adds $3 billion to the annual cost of health care in America. According to the department's study, an oversupply of surgeons and hospital beds, *as well as the* present system of hospital reimbursement, *encourages* excessive surgery. Proportionately, about *twice as much* surgery is performed in the United States *as in* England.

In response to the problem, the Department of Health has begun a program of asking all patients to get a second opinion before undergoing elective or nonemergency surgery.

A spokesperson for the American Medical Association called the government figures about unnecessary surgery "terribly exaggerated" and opposed any call for mandatory second opinions.

LISTENING TRANSCRIPT
FOR CHAPTER 13

Good evening and here's the news at five o'clock.

The United States Immigration and Naturalization Service announced today that it had arrested over 5,000 undocumented foreign workers at 560 work sites all over the country as part of its "Project Jobs" operation. The goal of the program is to open job opportunities for unemployed Americans. These jobs paid salaries slightly above the minimum wage. The raid was called an "unqualified success" by the head of the program.

However, the *President's* Commission on Immigration and Refugee Policy issued *a report* last week that concluded that there is *no proof* that illegal aliens *take away* jobs from American workers. *Although* there are as many as 6 *million* undocumented aliens *working in the* United States, the Commission found that *these* largely unskilled laborers *are not holding* jobs that Americans want.

The commission interviewed hundreds of Americans who had quit jobs filled previously by undocumented workers. The majority of the American workers found these jobs to be dead-end, demeaning, and poorly paying. Most of the American workers left these jobs to seek higher-paid employment and better working conditions.

LISTENING TRANSCRIPT
FOR CHAPTER 14

Good afternoon and here's the news at two o'clock.

One of television's largest *sponsors*, the Acme Drug Company, *has agreed* today to withdraw *its commercials* from four shows that a church group *has found* to be offensive. The Church of the Lord, headquartered in Abilene, Texas, *has waged an eight-month* "clean-up television" campaign which has attracted *more than a half million* followers in the United States and Canada. The church *had threatened* to boycott products sold by Acme Drug Company *unless the* company stopped advertising *on* television shows *containing* sex and violence.

And this morning five high school students have filed suit against the Long Island Tree School board for removing nine books from the school library. Represented by the New York Civil Liberties Union, the students are suing on the grounds that the school board's action violated their rights under the First Amendment. Stephen Pico, president of the student council and one of the plaintiffs in the suit, said that school should be the place to be exposed to a diversity of ideas. In response, the school board said that it had only removed "objectionable" books which were "anti-Christian, anti-Semitic, and just plain filthy."

Appendix II:
Answer Key

ANSWERS/CHAPTER 1

Test Your Comprehension

A: 1. F 2. F 3. F 4. T 5. T 6. F 7. F 8. F 9. T
B: 9
D. *Vocabulary 1:* 1. oblivious 2. mumbled 3. stoic 4. vowed 5. suppress 6. gossip 7. reprieve 8. dreaded 9. grasp 10. misconstrued
E. *Vocabulary 2:* 1. truth 2. puzzling 3. success 4. fluent 5. embarrassing 6. endurance 7. rigorous 8. assumption
G. *Vocabulary 4:* 1. few 2. most 3. in 4. listening, advice 5. principles 6. two-bedroom, suite, on

ANSWERS/CHAPTER 2

Test Your Comprehension

A: 1. T 2. F 3. F 4. F 5. T 6. F 7. F 8. F 9. T 10. T
B: 5
D. *Vocabulary 1:* 1. shabby 2. tougher 3. deter 4. reckless 5. clogged 6. fatally 7. flunked 8. dodge 9. cruise 10. ineffectual
E. *Vocabulary 2:* 1. offense 2. deterrence 3. notoriety 4. congested 5. renewing
G. *Vocabulary 4:* 1. took 2. million 3. few 4. a 5. the

ANSWERS/CHAPTER 3

Test Your Comprehension

A: 1. T 2. F 3. F 4. F 5. T 6. T 7. F 8. F 9. F
B: 6
D. *Vocabulary 1:* 1. bond 2. contempt 3. sentenced, life imprisonment 4. take the stand 5. latent, overt 6. appeal 7. overruled, cross examination 8. common-law 9. slur
E. *Vocabulary 2:* 1. dead 2. prosecuting 3. worth 4. racist 5. evident 6. confronted 7. conviction
G. *Vocabulary 4:* 1. borrow 2. death 3. 16-year-old 4. argue, 0 5. other

ANSWERS/CHAPTER 4

Test Your Comprehension

A: 1. F 2. T 3. T 4. T 5. T 6. F 7. F 8. F
B: 2
D. *Vocabulary 1:* 1. relegated 2. resolutely 3. sheepish 4. drafty 5. balk 6. puffing 7. ban 8. retort 9. submit 10. deprive
E. *Vocabulary 2:* 1. chosen 2. irritating 3. discriminatory 4. impressive 5. indulgent 6. impaired 7. hostility 8. productive 9. offense 10. absenteeism or absences
G. *Vocabulary 4:* 1. may be 2. billion 3. smoking 4. like 5. equipment

ANSWERS/CHAPTER 5

Test Your Comprehension

A: 1. F 2. T 3. T 4. F 5. T 6. T 7. T 8. F 9. F 10. F
B: 2
D. *Vocabulary 1:* 1. entangled 2. recalled 3. avid 4. scalded 5. potential 6. coroner 7. link 8. paranoid 9. acutely 10. lemon 11. underling
E. *Vocabulary 2:* 1. defective 2. productive 3. hazardous 4. safety 5. consciousness 6. dissatisfied 7. promoted
G. *Vocabulary 4:* 1. has 2. million, because, fall, a number 3. than 4. permit 5. making, major 6. a, Ø

ANSWERS/CHAPTER 6

Test Your Comprehension

A: 1. T 2. T 3. F 4. T 5. F 6. T 7. T 8. F 9. F 10. F
B: 4
D. *Vocabulary 1:* 1. pungent 2. grabbed 3. mobbed 4. sputtering 5. slammed 6. proprietor 7. scowled 8. messy 9. savoured
E. *Vocabulary 2:* 1. embarrassed 2. impressive 3. choice 4. confronted 5. sanitary 6. chaotic 7. tasty 8. reliant 9. courteous 10. air-conditioned
G. *Vocabulary 4:* 1. its 2. seated, 31-year-old 3. 30 years old 4. clash 5. rising 6. prove

ANSWERS/CHAPTER 7

Test Your Comprehension

A: 1. F 2. F 3. T 4. F 5. T 6. F 7. F 8. F
B: 5
D. *Vocabulary 1:* 1. flirted 2. incentive 3. infiltrated 4. exclusively 5. welders 6. disproportionate 7. snidely 8. fetch 9. turnabout 10. stigma
E. *Vocabulary 2:* 1. secretarial 2. sexually 3. research 4. economize 5. anesthetized 6. mistakenly 7. dominating 8. assertive
G. *Vocabulary 4:* 1. as 2. the most 3. quite, Ø 4. the 5. raised

ANSWERS/CHAPTER 8

Test Your Comprehension

A: 1. T 2. F 3. T 4. F 5. T 6. F 7. T 8. T
B: 1
D. *Vocabulary 1:* 1. stuck 2. tight 3. cramped 4. subsidized 5. took on 6. skyrocketed 7. yielded 8. peeked
E. *Vocabulary 2:* 1. worst 2. plumber 3. installation 4. rewarding 5. costly 6. socializing 7. rivalry 8. driven 9. married 10. subsidy
G. *Vocabulary 4:* 1. than 2. five-year 3. whose 4. it's 5. economics 6. parents'

ANSWERS/CHAPTER 9

Test Your Comprehension

A: 1. F 2. T 3. F 4. F 5. T 6. F 7. T 8. T 9. F 10. T
B: 2
D. *Vocabulary 1:* 1. peak 2. apprentice 3. zeal 4. grossly 5. self-made 6. permeated 7. nostalgic 8. commitment 9. widespread 10. indispensable
E. *Vocabulary 2:* 1. political 2. economical 3. lose 4. depth 5. led 6. literacy 7. critical 8. competent
G. *Vocabulary 4:* 1. million 2. numbers 3. whom 4. loss

ANSWERS/CHAPTER 10

Test Your Comprehension

A: 1. F 2. F 3. T 4. F 5. F 6. F 7. T 8. T 9. F
B: 3
D. *Vocabulary 1:* 1. poll 2. mimic 3. expatriate 4. recruit 5. carry on 6. vague 7. moonlighting 8. penniless 9. accosted 10. motive
E. *Vocabulary 2:* 1. studious 2. prestigious 3. notorious 4. critically 5. intentional 6. vaguest 7. occurrence 8. implied 9. swollen or swelling
G. *Vocabulary 4:* 1. on 2. Ø 3. as 4. lose 5. almost 6. may be 7. too

ANSWERS/CHAPTER 11

Test Your Comprehension

A: 1. F 2. T 3. F 4. F 5. T 6. F 7. F 8. T
B: 5
D. *Vocabulary 1:* 1. seizure 2. potent 3. circumstantial 4. contended 5. advocacy 6. misdemeanor 7. discernible 8. rigid 9. unattainable 10. felony
E. *Vocabulary 2:* 1. bulky 2. disputed 3. indictment 4. private 5. tolerance 6. rebellious
G. *Vocabulary 4:* 1. 50-pound, personal, sale 2. lies 3. effect 4. its, other

ANSWERS/CHAPTER 12

Test Your Comprehension

A: 1. F 2. T 3. F 4. T 5. F 6. F 7. T 8. T
B: 2
D. *Vocabulary 1:* 1. defy 2. injunction 3. barred 4. picket 5. resuscitate 6. ward 7. cutbacks 8. unauthorized 9. unethical 10. disclosure
E. *Vocabulary 2:* 1. volunteers 2. legalize 3. failure 4. permission 5. struck 6. negligent 7. suit 8. previously 9. medical
G. *Vocabulary 4:* 1. affected 2. equipment 3. made, save 4. patients', told, these

ANSWERS/CHAPTER 13

Test Your Comprehension

A: 1. T 2. F 3. F 4. T 5. T 6. F 7. T 8. F
B: 1
D. *Vocabulary 1:* 1. precocious 2. fickle 3. embittered 4. plump 5. improvised 6. grumpy 7. lap 8. shrieked 9. stitches 10. freelance
E. *Vocabulary 2:* 1. startled 2. prospective 3. ultimately 4. crushed 5. promotion 6. expertise
G. *Vocabulary 4:* 1. on 2. ∅, 30-year-old 3. anymore 4. role 5. exceeds 6. five-foot 7. being

ANSWERS/CHAPTER 14

Test Your Comprehension

A: 1. T 2. F 3. T 4. T 5. F 6. T 7. F 8. T
B: 1
D. *Vocabulary 1:* 1. tedious 2. narcotics 3. harsh 4. accessible 5. profusely 6. conceded 7. taboo 8. cringed 9. anguish 10. pejorative 11. inevitable 12. grasp 13. swarming
E. *Vocabulary 2:* 1. perception 2. ironic 3. harassed 4. cruelty 5. intimidated 6. outrageous 7. poisonous 8. dreadful 9. satirical
G. *Vocabulary 4:* 1. c 2. f 3. b 4. g 5. e 6. a 7. d